SECRETS OF THE C&O CANAL

Little-Known Stories & Hidden History Along the Potomac River

Other books by James Rada, Jr.

Non-Fiction

- Battlefield Angels: The Daughters of Charity Work as Civil War Nurses
- Beyond the Battlefield: Stories from Gettysburg's Rich History
- Clay Soldiers: One Marine's Story of War, Art, & Atomic Energy
- Echoes of War Drums: The Civil War in Mountain Maryland
- The Last to Fall: The 1922 March, Battles & Deaths of U.S. Marines at Gettysburg
- Looking Back: True Stories of Mountain Maryland
- Looking Back II: More True Stories of Mountain Maryland
- No North, No South: The Grand Reunion at the 50th Anniversary of the Battle of Gettysburg
- Saving Shallmar: Christmas Spirit in a Coal Town

Secrets Series

- Secrets of Catoctin Mountain: Little-Known Stories & Hidden History Along Catoctin Mountain
- Secrets of Garrett County: Little-Known Stories & Hidden History of Maryland's Westernmost County

Fiction

- Between Rail and River
- Canawlers
- Lock Ready
- October Mourning
- The Rain Man

CRITICAL ACCLAIM FOR THE WORKS OF JAMES RADA, JR.

The Last to Fall

"Authors Jim Rada and Richard Fulton have done an outstanding job of researching and chronicling this little-known story of those Marines in 1922, marking it as a significant moment in Marine Corps history."

- *GySgt. Thomas Williams*
Executive Director
U.S. Marine Corps Historical Company

"Original, unique, profusely illustrated throughout, exceptionally well researched, informed, informative, and a bit iconoclastic, 'The Last to Fall: The 1922 March, Battles, & Deaths of U.S. Marines at Gettysburg' will prove to be of enormous interest to military buffs and historians."

- *Small Press Bookwatch*

Saving Shallmar

"But Saving Shallmar's Christmas story is a tale of compassion and charity, and the will to help fellow human beings not only survive, but also be ready to spring into action when a new opportunity presents itself. Bittersweet yet heartwarming, Saving Shallmar is a wonderful Christmas season story for readers of all ages and backgrounds, highly recommended."

- *Small Press Bookwatch*

Battlefield Angels

"Rada describes women religious who selflessly performed life-saving work in often miserable conditions and thereby gained the admiration and respect of countless contemporaries. In so doing, Rada offers an appealing narrative and an entry point into the wealth of sources kept by the sisters."

- *Catholic News Service*

Between Rail and River

"The book is an enjoyable, clean family read, with characters young and old for a broad-based appeal to both teens and adults. Between Rail and River also provides a unique, regional appeal, as it teaches about a particular group of people, ordinary working 'canawlers' in a story that goes beyond the usual coverage of life during the Civil War."

- *Historical Fiction Review*

Canawlers

"A powerful, thoughtful and fascinating historical novel, Canawlers documents author James Rada, Jr. as a writer of considerable and deftly expressed storytelling talent."

- *Midwest Book Review*

"James Rada, of Cumberland, has written a historical novel for high-schoolers and adults, which relates the adventures, hardships and ultimate tragedy of a family of boaters on the C&O Canal. ... The tale moves quickly and should hold the attention of readers looking for an imaginative adventure set on the canal at a critical time in history."

- *Along the Towpath*

October Mourning

"This is a very good, and very easy to read, novel about a famous, yet unknown, bit of 20th Century American history. While reading this book, in your mind, replace all mentions of 'Spanish Flu' with 'bird flu.' Hmmm."

- *Reviewer's Bookwatch*

SECRETS OF THE C&O CANAL

Little-Known Stories & Hidden History
Along the Potomac River

by
James Rada, Jr.

LEGACY
PUBLISHING

A division of AIM Publishing Group

SECRETS OF THE C&O CANAL: LITTLE-KNOWN STORIES AND HIDDEN HISTORY ALONG THE POTOMAC RIVER

Published by Legacy Publishing, a division of AIM Publishing Group.
Gettysburg, Pennsylvania.

Printed in the United States of America.
First printing: February 2018.

ISBN 978-0-998554297

This is a collection previously published articles and new material.

Cover design by Grace Eyler.

LEGACY
PUBLISHING

315 Oak Lane • Gettysburg, Pennsylvania 17325

For Sam,
The engineer in the family
who can appreciate this engineering marvel.

CONTENTS

A Brief History of the Chesapeake and Ohio Canal........ 3
Building the Canal 9
How the Canal Helped Form the Federal Government 11
George Washington's Dream
of Making Water Run Uphill 17
What the C&O Might Have Been................................ 25
A Race From the Start 29
Coerced Labor on the Canal 39
The Engineering Marvel Hidden Under a Mountain 45
Expanding the C&O Canal 51
The Canal Snags on Point of Rocks............................. 61
Locks and Lockhouses.. 65
Celebrating the Opening of the C&O Canal 71
The War Between the States 75
The Real Mason Dixon Line... 77
From Building Boats to Healing Soldiers..................... 81
The Battle of Ball's Bluff 91
The Potomac Home Brigade... 95
Stanton's Navy... 99
C&O Canal President Imprisoned for Treason........... 105
The Canal in Operation... 107
More Than a Way to Move Coal 109
Are Two Boats Better Than One?............................... 115
The Georgetown Incline Plane 121
Coxey's Army Marches on Washington...................... 127
Labor Trouble on the C&O Canal 135
The Last Years 139
The Spong Family Tragedy 141

The Johnstown Flood's Cousin Nearly Killed the Canal 147
The B&O and C&O: Rivals and Associates 157
When the C&O Canal Closed 165
Once the Canal Closed 169
The Murders That Didn't Happen on the C&O Canal 171
Forging Through the Mountains 179
The Connection Between the JFK Assassination and the C&O Canal 183
Rethinking the C&O Canal 188
Acknowledgments 195
About the Author 197

A Brief History of the Chesapeake and Ohio Canal

Working on the Chesapeake & Ohio Canal meant that your life was connected to a stretch of water that was 60 feet wide and 184.5 miles long running from Cumberland, Md., to Georgetown in the District of Columbia. The path of the canal roughly followed the course of the Potomac River, which supplied the canal with the water that was its lifeblood.

The C&O Canal was the fulfillment of George Washington's dream to make water flow uphill. It was the first great national project, and it was a failure.

George Washington's dream

Long before Washington dreamed of an independent nation, he dreamed of making the Potomac River a navigable commerce route. Washington sought most of his life for a way to make eastward and westward river travel on the Potomac River possible. He wrote that a dependable trade route would "apply the cement of interest to bind all parts of the union together by indissoluble bonds, especially that part of it, which lies immediately west of us, with the middle states."

He helped form the Patowmack Company, which did build a short canal that allowed small vessels to skirt Great Falls, which was the major impediment to making the Potomac River navigable. It wasn't enough, though. The boats that came down the river were generally large log rafts. Once they reached Georgetown, their goods were delivered and the rafts broken up and the logs sold. And even these rafts could only travel the river during times of high water, otherwise they risked being grounded in shallows.

Washington died in 1799 without ever seeing the river become fully navigable.

The Great National Project

Decades after Washington's attempt to tame the Potomac River, America took an interest in canals that began with the success of the Erie Canal in New York. The federal government decided to undertake the construction of a canal to facilitate interstate commerce.

On July 4, 1828, President John Quincy Adams broke ground for the Chesapeake and Ohio Canal near the Great Falls in Maryland.

"The project contemplates a conquest over physical nature, such as has never yet been achieved by man. The wonders of the ancient world, the pyramids of Egypt, the Colossus of Rhodes, the temple at Ephesus, the mausoleum of Artemisia, the wall of China, sink into insignificance before it: —insignificance in the mass and momentum of human labor required for the execution—insignificance in comparison of the purposes to be accomplished by the work when executed," Adams said.

Then the President was given a shovel and attempted to turn the first spadeful of dirt. In an ominous turn of events, he hit rocky ground. So hard was the ground that the president wound up taking off his suit coat to wrestle a spadeful of earth from the rocks.

The C&O Canal was a construction and engineering challenging for its time. It involved more than simply digging a trench across level land and making it water tight. Boats traveling from Georgetown to Cumberland had to be lifted more than 600 feet on their westward journey.

The laborers were mainly imported Irishmen, who jumped at the chance to come to America, though they quickly found the work unsatisfying. It was hard and the tools were picks, shovels, horses and black powder.

When completed, the canal had eleven aqueducts, seventy-four lift locks, 160 culverts, and twelve river feeder locks and guard locks.

The problem was that by the time the canal reached Cumberland in 1850, the Baltimore and Ohio Railroad had already been there eight years, although both projects had started on the same day in 1828.

The final cost of the C&O Canal was $14 million or $9.5 million more than estimated. According to Elizabeth Kytle in *Home on the Canal*, as a portion of the gross national project, building the C&O Canal was the equivalent to putting a man on the moon.

Canawling

Boatmen on the C&O Canal called themselves canallers, though to many people it sounded like they were saying "canawlers."

Mules walked along the towpath pulling the canal boats. A mule driver was one of the first jobs a youngster could have on the canal. J.P. Mose began working on the canal as a driver when he was eight years old.

"I wasn't tall enough to reach up [to a mule's head]. They had a little strap I'd get hold of to stop him and start him," Mose said in an interview before he died.

Steering a canal boat was trickier. The boat was slow to respond to a change of direction and navigating around other boats and into the locks took some skill. Even so, boys and girls as young as 12 or 13 were often given the job steering the boat.

For many canallers, boating was a family business. Every job that could be done by a family member meant that a hired hand wouldn't be needed.

Families could even live on the canal boat, though it was cramped quarters. Canal boats were ninety-two-feet-long, but most of that space was dedicated to holds to carry 120 tons of coal.

Canal boats had three cabins. The mule stable was fore and housed the mules that weren't pulling the canal boat. The hay house was mid-ship. It held hay for the mules and could also serve as a sleeping area. The family cabin was aft. It was about 10 feet square and contained beds, table, stove and a pantry.

The Beginning of the End

In the early years, the B&O Railroad and C&O Canal fought for business. The railroad moved faster, but canal boats could carry more than the early trains.

Following the Civil War, the canal entered its golden age, where the canal company actually began to see profits. For a few years, from 1876 to 1889, six passenger steamers operated on the canal.

Then the same storm that caused the 1889 Johnstown Flood hit the region causing massive flooding to the Potomac River and damaging the C&O Canal. The flooding not only destroyed portions of the canal, but the floodwaters carried some canal boats far inland and smashed others against the aqueducts, according to the *Cumberland Evening Times*.

The damage was so great that the canal went into receivership only to be taken over by its rival the B&O Railroad. The railroad had been purchasing many of the bonds issued on behalf of the canal, so much so that it became the majority bondholder of the C&O Canal when the canal went bankrupt.

"Seemingly it would be the one to decide the future of its former great rival. The railroad company weighed the comparative costs of a forced sale to a possible competitor (or to itself at a high price) and the restoration of the canal at its own expense. It chose the latter course," Walter Sanderlin wrote in *The Great National Project*.

The canal never truly showed a profit after 1890; however, running the canal at a profit was required by the terms of the receivership or it would be sold. The B&O Railroad created the C&O Transportation Company to create an agreement that would allow the C&O Canal to show a paper profit.

In 1902, the Consolidation Coal Company, which was owned by the B&O, formed the Canal Towage Company. This changed the life on the canal. Captains became employees of the Canal Towage Company and had their boats provided to them by the company. The once-colorful boats with fanciful names now became uniform with only a number identifying one boat from another.

After two spring floods severely damaged the canal in 1924, it closed for good.

Many of its secrets are forgotten, but *Secrets of the C&O Canal* has uncovered some of the hidden history and little-known stories of the C&O Canal.

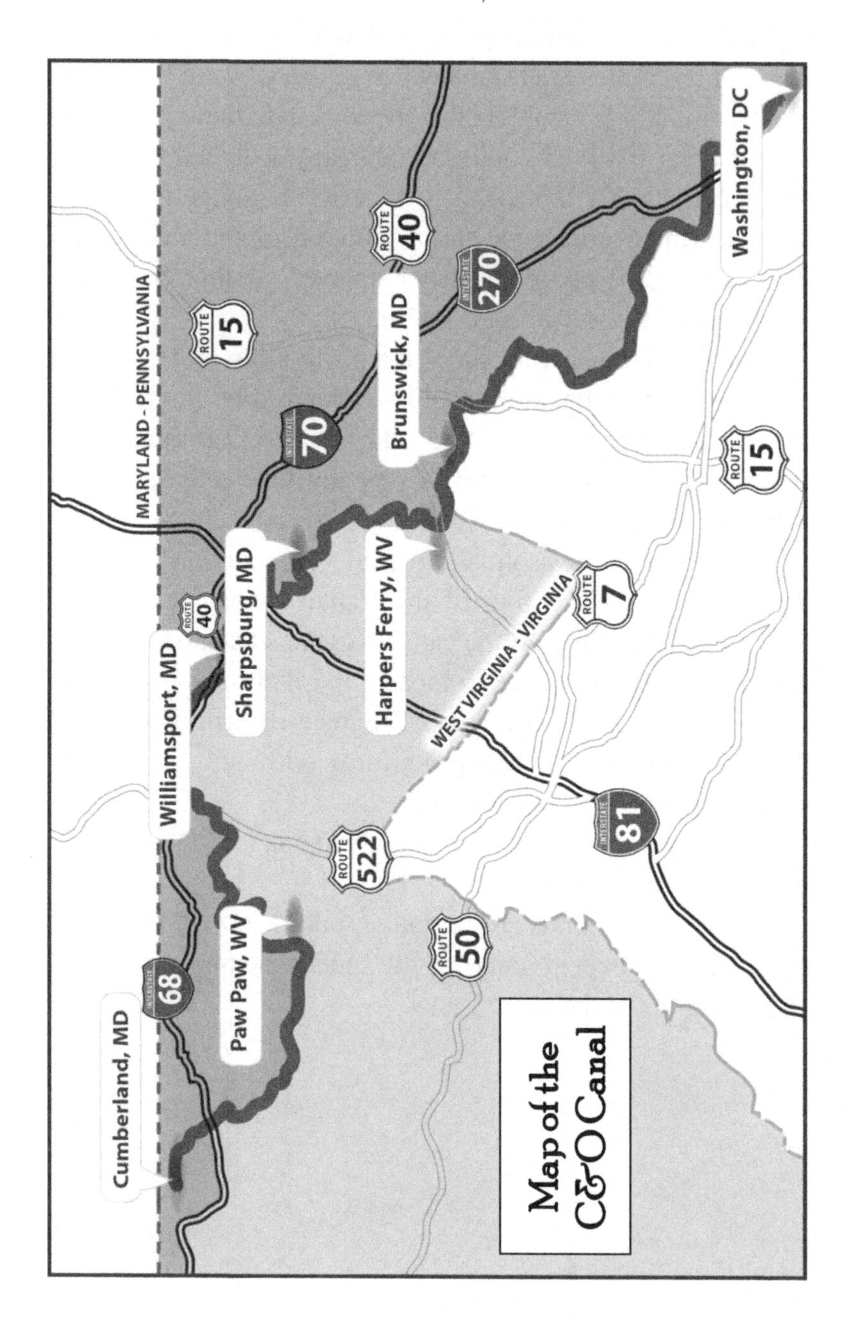
Map of the C&O Canal
Cumberland, MD
Paw Paw, WV
Williamsport, MD
Sharpsburg, MD
Harpers Ferry, WV
Brunswick, MD
Washington, DC
MARYLAND - PENNSYLVANIA
WEST VIRGINIA - VIRGINIA
68
70
81
270
ROUTE 15
ROUTE 40
ROUTE 40
ROUTE 522
ROUTE 50
ROUTE 7
ROUTE 15

Building the Canal

How the Canal Helped Form the Federal Government

Before construction could be started on George Washington's Patowmack Company locks, Maryland and Virginia had to work out issues about each state's claim to the Potomac River. Lord Baltimore's 1632 grant, which created Maryland, established its southern boundary as the southern shore of the river, meaning that Maryland controlled all of the river. However, there was also reference in the grant that gave Virginia free navigation and use of the river.

Because the locks of the Patowmack Company were on the Virginia shore and the company also needed to make improvements to the river to make it navigable, Maryland's cooperation was needed but not forthcoming.

Washington's engineer for the project, John Ballendine ran a notice in the October 1775 *Virginia Gazette* that read, in part, "The necessity of a Maryland Act of Assembly cooperating with one passed in Virginia, and which I have not yet been able to obtain, has obliged me to decline it for the present."

In 1785, both sides agreed to meet and selected commissioners to represent their interests. The Maryland commissioners suggested the time and place for the meeting and believed that the Virginia delegation was in agreement.

Amid a heavy snowstorm on March 20, 1785, the Maryland commissioners, made up of Samuel Chase, Daniel of St.

Thomas Jenifer, and Thomas Stone, arrived at the tavern in Alexandria where the meeting was to take place. Only there was no Virginia delegation to meet them.

The Virginia delegation was made up of Alexander Henderson and George Mason. James Madison and Edmund Randolph had been appointed but were not sufficiently notified of their appointments to make the meeting.

"We waited some days, expecting your arrival at Alexandria, when I received a letter from the attorney upon other business, without mentioning a word of the meeting or of the Assembly's appointment. This convinced me that there must have been some blunder or neglect in some of the public offices in not giving the proper notification to the Virginia commissioners," George Mason wrote to the Virginia Assembly.

He had been made aware of the meeting when two members of the Maryland delegation stopped by to visit with him on their way to Alexandria. He then took it upon himself to begin negotiations.

To try and make up for Virginia's blunder to soothe the Maryland delegation, Washington offered the hospitality of Mount Vernon in place of the tavern. The Marylanders accepted.

Once in the relaxed atmosphere of Washington's home with plenty of food and wine, progress was made and agreement reached. Maryland maintained its control of the river, but Virginia was allowed free access. Tolls, tariffs, fishing rights, the common value of currency, and naval protection of the river were all agreed upon. The states also agreed to share the costs of any navigational aids that needed to be constructed for the river.

More importantly, the commissioners realized that this wasn't a situation where there would be a winner and a loser. By cooperating, both states would see benefits.

Mount Vernon on the Potomac River. It was here that a delegation of commissioners from and Virginia and Maryland met to decide how the river would be controlled.

In his letter to the legislature, Mason wrote, "We flatter ourselves that, in the execution of this important trust, the commissioners have consulted the true interest of both governments, in a compact of such just and mutual principles, that, executed with good faith, will perpetuate harmony, friendship, and good offices between the two States, so essential to the prosperity and happiness of their people. In the conference on the subject of our appointment, several matters occurred to the commissioners, which they conceived very important to the commerce of the two States; and which, with all deference, we take the liberty to communicate."

Called the Mount Vernon Conference, the agreement became a model of how state governments of the new country could work together.

"Inspired, perhaps, by Washington's vision of a powerful empire, they opened their eyes to the possibility that interstate cooperation could be extended beyond the parochial concerns of the Potomoac. Why not bring in the other neighboring states?" Joel Achenbach wrote in *The Grand Idea: George Washington's Potomac and the Race to the West.*

The commissioners decided that they would meet the following year in Annapolis and invite delegations from all of the states to work out issues of mutual interest. The meeting was set to be held in George Mann's Tavern on September 11, 1786, and was titled "A Meeting of Commissioners to Remedy Defects of the Federal Government."

George Washington's Mount Vernon Conference led to the First Constitutional Convention and the creation of the U.S. Constitution. Photo courtesy of Library of Congress.

Unfortunately, when the date for the meeting came, only five states were represented, and oddly enough, George Washington, who had facilitated the first meeting was not included in the Virginia delegation. Four other states had actually appointed delegates, but they either arrived too late or did not attend at all. Enough discussion took place, though, to realize that the idea of a meeting of the states had merit.

The Annapolis meeting was adjourned since no quorum was present, but it was agreed to meet the following year in Philadelphia. Also, the topics that the delegation wanted to discuss were broadened.

On May 1, 1787, all of the colonies had representatives in Philadelphia at what became the First Constitutional Convention and led to the creation of the United States Constitution, the framework of the United States government.

"Washington's Potomac scheme culminated in something entirely different from, and far more important than, a navigable river. In pursuit of his goal, Washington set in motion a series of meetings that would lead to the creation of a document that would endure long after the skirting canal at Great Falls had been abandoned," Achenbach wrote.

George Washington's Dream of Making Water Run Uphill

George Washington was 22 years old in 1754. He journeyed to the Great Falls, a short trip from his Mount Vernon estate, and looked on the massive waterfall that made the Potomac River impassable. He began to think about ways a boat could travel around those falls and continue upstream or pass downstream without danger. It was a problem that wouldn't be solved until he had more than doubled in age.

The Potomac River builds up speed on its way east from its mixing with the Shenandoah River at Harpers Ferry. Harpers Ferry has rapids formed not only from the mixing of the two rivers from the parallel ledges of rock beneath the water.

At Great Falls, the Potomac River drops nearly seventy-six feet over 1,200 yards. It tumbles and froths over the steep and jagged rocks that make up twenty separate waterfalls and then all that force is channeled through the Mather Gorge, where the river narrows from 1,000-feet wide to sixty feet.

Washington had shot the Harpers Ferry rapids in a canoe during one of his trips on the Potomac, but traveling the river by boat at Great Falls was impossible…or so it appeared at the time. While a boat might navigate the rapids, could any craft survive a fall of seventy-six feet onto rock?

To this point in history, anyone who wanted to use the river had to beach their boats above the falls, unload its contents, carry the contents and boat around the falls, and reload the boat below the falls. It was a long and cumbersome process and one that limited the cargo that could be carried downriver.

A portion of Great Falls in the Potomac River that made the waterway unnavigable for boats until the creation of the Patowmack Company.

But Washington believed that if the river could be improved…if it could be made navigable, the benefits to Virginia would be great as cities like Alexandria could become shipping ports to the West.

From Great Falls east, one could navigate the river by boat about fourteen miles to Georgetown. From Great Falls west, one could navigate the river by boat about eight miles to the Seneca rapids. And beyond that, additional falls and rapids would need to be overcome to navigate the river further west.

That could happen, though and when it did, the river would be open for navigation to Cumberland.

But it was at Great Falls that would be the major sticking point to making the Potomac River navigable.

The seal of George Washington's Patowmack Company. Photo courtesy of the National Park Service.

The ground is hard and granite-like. Washington had walked the cliffs and felt the hardness of the stone beneath his boots. The rock would not give easily. It hadn't worn away after all the hundreds of thousands of years this river must have worn on it.

After the Revolutionary War, George Washington was considered a hero and military genius by the young United

States, but the Great Falls caused him hesitation because he was not sure how to conquer it in order to make his dream come true. He only knew it must be conquered for the future of his country lay to the west of the Allegheny Mountains.

A dependable and safe transportation route would join the eastern states with the western lands and "to apply the cement of interest to bind all parts of the union together by indissoluble bonds, especially that part of it, which lies immediately west of us, with the middle states," Washington wrote.

One man had already begun to overcome some of the problems at Great Falls. John Ballendine had built a dam and small skirting canal around Little Falls to help power his grist mill. Around 1770, Ballendine had persuaded Washington and others to help fund construction of the skirting canal.

While the grist mill didn't interest Washington much, the skirting canal did and it would lead to his first presidency…not of the United States, but of the Patowmack Company.

Washington became president of the Patowmack Company in January 1785, the announcement was not official until May. He was to receive the almost token salary of thirty shillings a year as president.

According to the terms of its charter, the purpose of the Patowmack Company was the opening of the Potomac River to the highest point of permanent navigation. The minimum goal was to reach Fort Cumberland in Western Maryland, at which point a connection would be made with the improved Braddock Road, providing access to the rapidly filling lands tapped by the Ohio and its tributaries. The intention was to deepen the river channel and cut canals around the falls and rapids to permit the passage of boats capable of carrying fifty barrels of flour in the driest seasons.

While Washington's support of the project was invaluable, he was a visionary, not an engineer. Notices were placed in newspapers in Baltimore and Philadelphia. The company offered generous daily rations of: 1 lb. of salt pork, 1.25 lb. of salt beef, or 1.5 lb. of fresh beef or mutton, 1.5 lb. of flour or bread, and 3 gills of rum.

This was not enough to attract laborers in sufficient quantities. Not because the rations weren't liberal. There just weren't enough hands in the predominantly agricultural area to meet the demands of the project. In a bit of desperation, the company directors began to use indentured servants and slaves to meet the labor needs.

Meanwhile, with the proper capital, work began on improving the river. Two teams of men were hired to begin work. One team worked between Harpers Ferry and Great Falls and the other team worked on the river above Harpers Ferry.

The other problem the Patowmack Company ran into was that no one in America knew how to build a canal. Finding an engineer to head the project was just as hard as finding enough laborers. No suitable candidates were found to lead the project by July and so "local talent of doubtful quality was tried," according to the company's records. Then Washington called on the man who seemed not only to have the vision but the ability to accomplish the project…James Rumsey.

Besides being a mechanical engineer, Rumsey is best known for demonstrating a steam-propelled boat on the Potomac River near Shepherdstown in 1786, well before Robert Fulton, who was actually an apprentice to Rumsey. Rumsey's steamboat used a pump driven by steam power that ejected water from the stern, propelling the boat forward.

Rumsey worked on trying to clear the river for about a year. He became very frustrated with the work and quality of workers. He told the company directors that he would resign if not given a raise. He wasn't, and so he resigned. Steward Richardson took over as the engineer following Rumsey's departure.

A young George Washington had canoed the Potomac River and dreamed of opening it up for commerce. Photo courtesy of the Library of Congress.

With the creation of the Constitution of the United States, which the Patowmack Company, had played a small part in starting, a president was required to head the federal government. Though a presidential election was required, the choice was obvious. The nation chose not only the hero of the Revolution, but a man who had already served as president twice. First as President of the Patowmack Company and then as President of the First Continental Congress.

Even after he was unknowingly elected president on February 4, 1789, Washington still pursued his interest in improving the Potomac River, not knowing word was on its way south from New York that he had been elected. He wrote to Thomas Jefferson about new maps he had received that indicated the portages for between the eastern and western waters might be shorter than expected.

The remains of the skirting locks on the Virginia side of the Potomac River were part of the Patowmack Company.

Once Washington became President of the United States, work did not stop on the canal. It continued under the supervision of James Smith who had replaced the incompetent Steward Richardson in 1788.

Washington still attended meetings of the Patowmack Company, which is how he knew in February 1798, the company needed $40,000 to finish the Great Falls locks. He loaned the company $3,498.

In the last year of his life, Washington seemed to regret that he had put aside the work on the Potomac River to serve his country in other ways.

The skirting canals around Great Falls were finished and the river navigable from Georgetown to Cumberland in 1802. Washingon's dream had been realized, but he did not live to see it fulfilled. He died in 1799.

What the C&O Canal Might Have Been

It is often stated that the ultimate goal of the Chesapeake and Ohio Canal was to reach the Ohio River so that cargo could be transported from the Chesapeake Bay to Pittsburgh, Pa., and possibly the Mississippi River. After a time, this was true, but before construction on the canal started, it had another destination.

The Erie Canal, which ran 363 miles from Albany, N.Y., to Buffalo, N.Y., opened in 1821 and was a financial success. It connected navigable waterways so that cargo could be transported from the ports in New York City to the Great Lakes.

"The Erie canal is a lasting monument of the wisdom, patriotism, and public spirit of the state of New York and has rendered certain, what was before problematical; it has removed doubts of skepticism itself, and stands a splendid example to the world, of what may be done in the way of Internal Improvements," the Convention for the Promotion of Internal Improvement reported in 1826.

This convention was held in Baltimore to garner public support for the canal project and a plan for where it would go and how it might be funded. Oddly, the president of the convention was Charles Carroll, at one time the richest man in the country. By the time the construction of the canal started in 1828, he had thrown his support behind the Baltimore and Ohio Railroad rather than the canal.

The Erie Canal was also seen as depriving Maryland from some of its wagon traffic along the National Road, which had opened from Cumberland, Md., to Vandalia, Ill., in 1811.

These early plans for the C&O Canal also called for a lateral canal to run from Baltimore and intersect the C&O Canal in Frederick County. This would have opened up the Port of Baltimore and perhaps even the Susquehanna River to canal navigation to western cities.

"Whilst the trade between the Atlantic and the west, was carried on by wagons, she participated largely in it, but the fact cannot be concealed, that the facilities to transportation offered by the Erie canal, are calculated to deprive her of it," the convention committee reported.

With the talk of building a canal through Maryland that was backed by the federal government, Maryland businessmen and legislators saw a chance to regain its lost business. The committee called the canal an "object of the first magnitude in this state, in an agricultural, commercial, and political point of view."

So enamored were state officials with the idea of having a canal as successful as the Erie in their state that they were willing to give up the wagon traffic in favor of canal boats. "When it is considered that the expense of transportation, by land, is more than twenty-five times greater than by the canal, it must be obvious to all reflecting minds, that there can be no competition between land and water carriage. – The wagon trade must be abandoned," according to the convention report. For instance, the report said that the cost of transporting a barrel of flour from Hagerstown to Baltimore was never less than $1 and usually a $1.25. That same flour transported by canal would cost 5 cents plus tolls.

The convention committee recommended that the ultimate destination of C&O Canal be Lake Erie, which is where the Erie Canal ultimately ended.

The Erie Canal as it passes through Rochester, N.Y. Photo courtesy of the Library of Congress.

The convention report stated that the distance from New York City to Lake Erie was 513 miles, of which 150 miles was river navigation. From Lake Erie to where the committee was recommending that the C&O Canal enter the lake was another 200 miles. By contrast, the distance from Baltimore to Lake Erie along the recommended route was 510 miles.

The report stated, "now if it be conceded, that the Erie canal will command the trade of the country on the north of the canal line, and also some distance on the south of it, it must be admitted that the Chesapeake and Ohio canal will command the trade of the country to the south of the canal line, which includes four fifths of the lake country, the states of Ohio, Indiana, and Illinois, part of Pennsylvania, Virginia, and Kentucky, and indeed, all the country whose trade is not exclusively confined to New Orleans."

For the ports further south from Buffalo, such as Pittsburgh and New Orleans, La., the mileage difference only grew in favor of the C&O Canal.

The committee whole-heartedly supported the construction of the canal. It also wanted to have the lateral canal built along the Patapsco River from Baltimore. The problem came with the price tag for the project. It was estimated that it would cost $22 million to build a canal from Baltimore to Lake Erie. This is roughly $600 million in 2016 dollars.

Both officials and the public balked at this price. It wasn't until the project was scaled down to a smaller canal from Georgetown to Cumberland for $4.5 million that the federal government felt the project was affordable.

A Race From The Start

The weather in the Washington D.C. area on July 4 was sunny and pleasant, similar to that in Baltimore, which wasn't surprising given their proximity to one another. The nation's capital was but forty miles from Baltimore, a day's ride by coach.

Another similarity between the locations was that they were both hosting historic groundbreakings for a large-scale transportation project that would allow eastern merchants to get their products to and from the underserved western markets.

While the Baltimore and Ohio Railroad was a private-sector project, the Chesapeake and Ohio Canal had the support, and to some extent, funding of the United States government.

Charles Carroll, the last surviving signer of the Declaration of Independence and one of the richest men in the country, had been an early supporter of the canal. He had subscribed 1,000 pounds sterling to the project in 1772 when the canal was the goal of Patowmack Company and in 1784, he served on the board of directors for the company along with George Washington.

Carroll's opinion about the canal had changed since that time. Not only was he not on hand for this historic groundbreaking; he was in Baltimore laying the first stone for a railroad.

He now believed that the Potomac River's power would be best used as the power source for mills. As for transporting goods, he believed a railroad from Great Falls to various points would be the better answer to navigating the falls. He threw his support behind the Baltimore and Ohio Railroad project.

The laying of the cornerstone for the Baltimore and Ohio Railroad on July 4, 1828. Photo courtesy of Wikimedia Commons.

So while Carroll was celebrating the start of the new railroad, President John Quincy Adams, son of the second President of the United States, was to be the guest of honor at the canal's groundbreaking to represent the country's interest in the project.

Like Carroll, Adams was a supporter of "internal improvements" for the young country. He had seen the value of canals while living in the Netherlands as a boy of thirteen and a man of twenty-seven. Adams' friend and supporter

William Seward, a future Secretary of State under Abraham Lincoln wrote in *Life and Public Services of John Quincy Adams:*

> "He recommended the opening of national roads and canals—the improvement of navigation of rivers, and the safety of harbors—the survey of our coasts, the erection of light houses, piers, and breakwaters. Whatever tended to facilitate communication and transportation between extreme portions of the Union—to bring the people of distant sections into a more direct intercourse with each other, and bind them together by ties of a business, social and friendly nature—to promote enterprise, industry and enlarged views of national and individual posterity—obtained his earnest sanction and recommendation."

In part, perhaps, his strong support came from the fact that when his father was dying two years before, Adams had immediately started from Washington to his hometown of Quincy, Massachusetts, a distance of 446 miles. The journey took him five days and the President was not only not by his father's side when John Adams died, John Quincy missed his father's funeral as well. Americans needed a faster form of travel.

In supporting the canal, it was the hope of Adams and the Congress that the Chesapeake and Ohio Canal would prove to be an even bigger economic boon than the government's other transportation project, the National Pike. In this, Adams differed from Carroll who thought it would better to harness the Potomac River's power to run mills not transport goods.

Construction of the National Pike began in 1811. It was a smooth, wide road that traveled over the mountains from

Cumberland, Md., to Wheeling, Va., and the Ohio River. The road reached there in 1817, allowing a fairly easy east-west route across the growing country.

The benefit of the canal was in the low cost to ship goods. Before the Erie Canal had been completed in 1825, it had cost $100 to ship a ton of goods over the roads from Buffalo, N.Y., to New York City and took twenty days. With the opening of the canal, the shipping cost dropped to $10 to $12 per ton and eight days.

Given the government's support of the project, it was not surprising to find a number of government officials, along with President John Quincy Adams, in attendance with the canal directors at breakfast at the Union Hotel on July 4, 1828. The mayors and committees of Washington, Georgetown and Alexandria attended, as well as federal officials, foreign government representatives, and other invited persons.

One of those invited persons was Adams' son, John, twenty-five years old at the time. The younger Adams served as his father's private secretary. John Quincy hoped his sons would follow in the footsteps of their father and grandfather and devote their lives to public service. In the case of John Adams II, he was beginning to follow in the footsteps of his father's younger brother Thomas Boylston Adams on the road to alcoholism.

The Chesapeake and Ohio Canal directors had selected the date for the groundbreaking based on tradition. Many of the major canals in the country had started on Independence Day. The Erie Canal broke ground on July 4, 1817. The Ohio and Erie Canal began on July 4, 1825 and the Pennsylvania Grand Canal on July 4, 1826. And the Chesapeake and Ohio Canal would begin on July 4, 1828.

Around 8 a.m. as the parade in Baltimore celebrating the

beginning of the B&O Railroad was officially starting, the U.S. Marine Corp Band started playing "Hail to the Chief."

Though the song had first been playing in the United States in 1812, this was the first time the song that would become known as the song that announced the President's arrival was played for a president. James Sanderson originally composed the song as part of a stage adaptation of Sir Walter Scott's "The Lady of the Lake." The song referred to not the Commander in Chief but a Scottish chieftain.

John Quincy Adams, the president of the United States, was a strong supporter of the C&O Canal. Photo courtesy of Wikimedia Commons.

The band led the smaller parade of dignitaries from the hotel in Georgetown to High Street Wharf. The group boarded the steamboat *Surprise* and two others, especially provided for the occasion.

The three steamboats, followed by a line of barges and other boats headed upriver "coursing the wild margin of what was once the Virginia Shore—still bordered, as when it came from the hands of its Maker, with primitive rocks, and crowned with the luxuriant and diversified foliage of its natural forest. A kindly sky shed its refreshing influence over the water, whose surface the West wind gently ruffled. The sun shone now and then from the clear blue Heavens through fleecy clouds," according to the *National Daily Intelligencer*.

Crowds also followed the path of the boats from the shore, moving in a growing in a snowball of humanity as the boats moved further west.

The *Surprise* stopped at Lock Cove, where the skirting canal around Little Falls was located on the Virginia side of the river. The group boarded canal boats and traveled through the old canal. They moved west for a few miles until they reached the head of Little Falls.

A large crowd of about 2,000 people had already gathered by the time the dignitaries arrived. With the Marine Band leading the way, two companies of riflemen fired a salute as Adams arrived.

The crowd created a large wheel around the spot of ground marked by Benjamin Wright, engineer for the canal company, "on a spot where little more than a century ago the painted savage held his nightly orgies," Seward wrote. Into the center of the wheel walked the group of dignitaries.

The ceremonial spade was selected and handed to Charles Mercer, president of the canal company. "At that moment the sun shone out from behind a cloud, giving an appearance of the highest animation to the scene," Seward wrote.

Mercer said to the crowd, "Fellow-citizens: There are moments in the progress of time which are the counters of whole ages. There are events, the monuments of which, surviving every other memorial of human existence, eternize the nation to whose history they belong, after all other vestiges of its glory have disappeared from the globe. At such a moment have we now arrived. Such a monument we are now to found."

The president of the Chesapeake and Ohio Canal Company handed President Adams the spade; "this humble instrument of rural labor, a symbol of the favorite occupation of our countrymen."

Adams compared the groundbreaking of the canal to the fulfillment of America as an "empire of learning and the arts" as foretold by Berkley, bishop of Cloyne. Adams said such a fulfillment came in three parts, each more difficult than the prior: achieving self-government, creation of the union of states and improvement of its own condition. It is this third step "more arduous still than either or both of the others" that Adams said the C&O Canal was a part.

> "That for the commencement of which we are here assembled is eminent among the number. The project contemplates a conquest over physical nature, such as has never yet been achieved by man. The wonders of the ancient world, the pyramids of Egypt, the Colossus of Rhodes, the temple at Ephesus, the mausoleum of Artemisia, the wall of China, sink into insignificance before it: --insignificance in the mass and momentum of human labor required for the execution—insignificance in comparison of the purposes to be accomplished by the work when executed."

And after a few more comments, Adams dug a spadeful of ground from the earth.

Or rather, he tried to.

The spade struck a root.

He tried again and "after repeating the stroke three or four times without making an impression."

Adams wrote of his efforts:

> "The incident that chiefly relieved me was the obstacle of the stump, which met and resisted the spade, and my casting off my coat to overcome the resistance. It struck the eye and fancy of the spectators more than all the flowers of rhetoric in my speech, and diverted their attention from the stammering and hesitation of a deficient memory."

Indeed, the crowd loved the display. They might not be able to hear the speeches, but they could see what was happening in front of them. The crowd cheered Adams on as he drove the spade into the ground once more. The cheers grew even louder as he finally managed to turn a spade full of earth.

"And that was about as close as John Quincy Adams ever came to pleasing a crowd who had come to see their president," wrote biographer Robert Remini.

The cheers certainly would have strengthened Adams' resolve and gladdened his heart, for his had not been a popular presidency. The presidential election of 1824 had been spirited and contentious between Adams, vice president to James Monroe; Andrew Jackson, war hero from the War of 1812; Henry Clay, a popular orator and Speaker of the House of Representatives and William Crawford, chosen to represent the southern states. Since all the candidates entertained similar views, the campaign had been personal as each candidate sought to set himself apart from his competitors.

When the electoral votes had been counted Jackson had received ninety-nine, Adams received eighty-four, Crawford received forty-one and Clay received thirty-seven. However, since there were 261 electoral votes, no candidate received the majority needed to become President.

Based on the twelfth amendment to U.S. Constitution, the top three electoral vote getters names were sent to the U.S. House of Representatives to be voted upon. Though Henry Clay came in third in the popular vote, he was fourth in the electoral vote. Hence, while his name was not on the ballot in the House, he had a say in the election in his role as Speaker of the House.

The election went to the House of Representatives on February 9, 1825. The House convened earlier than usual and the building was filled to capacity with spectators. All but one of the representatives was present.

The members of the Senate entered the chamber of the House of Representatives. John Galliard, president of the Senate rose and said no candidate had received a majority electoral votes and that Adams, Jackson and Crawford had received the most.

While the person who would be president was unknown, it was announced that John C. Calhoun of South Carolina had received 182 electoral votes and would be named vice president.

After the senators left, the House took its vote. From this vote, Adams received thirteen, Jackson received seven and Crawford received four.

Based on this, John Quincy became the first president who had not had a role in the War of Independence. He also had a smaller mandate than his father's three electoral vote win over Thomas Jefferson in 1796. American citizens knew John Quincy was not their choice for President and politicians knew Adams did not have a broad base of support. His presidency had been a contentious and somewhat, unpopular one. He had received few popular outpourings of popular support from the American people as he heard at the canal groundbreaking.

Once Adams had turned a spadeful of dirt, he put his coat back on and spoke to the crowd once again.

Following his speech, the other dignitaries scooped up their own spadeful of earth and dumped it into a wheelbarrow.

Following the groundbreaking, the group rested under a tent for a short time before they retraced their path back to Georgetown. On the deck of the steamboat, Adams was asked to make a toast as the group prepared to drink. The president raised his glass and said, "The Chesapeake and Ohio Canal: perseverance." The steamboat reached Davidson's Wharf around 2:30 p.m. where Adams climbed into his carriage and headed home.

Historian and professor George Washington Ward would write of the day's events in 1899, "Thus were inaugurated about the same hour and scarcely more than forty miles apart two works destined by their situation to decide for the world whether the transportation of the future was to be by canal or railroad."

The race was on!

Coerced Labor on the Canal

Although the Chesapeake and Ohio Canal wasn't built by slaves, it came close. The C&O Canal Company, in desperate need of laborers, began importing men from Europe as indentured workers.

The canal had labor troubles from the start. Besides the canal, the Baltimore and Ohio Railroad was looking for laborers as were other canal and railroad projects in the region, such as the Pennsylvania Main Line Canal. Workers had a choice of where they would work and "few could be attracted to it because of the reputation of the Potomac for ill health during the long hot and humid summer," Harlan Unrau wrote in *Historic Resource Study: Chesapeake and Ohio Canal.*

In the canal company's first annual report in June of 1829, it was noted that 2,113 men and boys were working on the canal, but the "number necessary to complete the canal under contract, in the time specified in the several contracts, cannot be short of 6,000."

Not only did the contractors doing the building have trouble finding enough labor, the laws of supply and demand meant that the more scarce laborers became, the higher the wages the existing laborers could command. At the beginning of the work, laborers were being paid $8 to $10 a month, but six months later in the summer of 1829, the same laborer could earn $12 to $13 a month. This drove up the cost of the project.

The scarcity of workers sometimes meant laborers who otherwise might not be able to find work were hired. W.

Robert Leckie, an masonry inspector for the canal, wrote in his notes, "Contractors and masons seem totally ignorant of what they should know, have neither skills nor tools to work with, everything done carelessly, and no attention paid to the mixing of the mortar."

One of the African American boatmen on the C&O Canal feeds his mules. This boat may have been captained by an African American because the other two people on the boat also appear to be African Americans. Photo courtesy of the National Park Service.

These conditions forced the canal company to start advertising for laborers in Europe. Newspaper ads ran in Great Britain, Germany, Ireland, and the Netherlands promising workers three meals a days with plenty of meat, bread, and vegetables. They were also receive a "reasonable allowance" of liquor. They would also be paid $8 to $12 a month ($20 a month for stone masons).

Then, because they still needed more men, the canal company decided to start using indentured servants. On January 31, 1829, the company made an agreement with Henry Richards to act as their agent in Great Britain to hire the needed men. The company agreed to pay the transportation costs of the workers to Baltimore for three months (78 days) of indentured servitude. They would also receive the same food rations as hired laborers, but they did not have to pay their board. The indentured workers also agreed to work on the canal for a year after their indentures ended, for which they would be paid the prevailing wage.

Despite their contracts, some of the workers fled into the countryside when they arrived. Others were lured away by better offers from the B&O Railroad. These men, if found, could be arrested and imprisoned for failing to live up their contracts.

For its part, the Canal Company might have lived up to the letter of its obligation but not much more. Living conditions for the workers were considered deplorable. Frances Milton Trollope wrote in *Domestic Manners of the Americans* about the canal laborers she saw. "There is a strong feeling against the Irish in every part of the Union, but they will do twice as much work as a Negro, and therefore they are employed. When they fall sick, they may, and must look with envy on the slaves around them; for they are cared for; for they are watched and physicked, as a valuable horse is watched and physicked: not so with the Irishman: he is literally thrown on one side, and a new comer takes his place."

Indentured servants turned out to be more trouble than aid for the canal company. The company started bringing them to America in August 1920 but stopped in October 1829.

This brings up whether there were slaves who actually

helped construct the C&O Canal as they did the Patowmack canal.

COMMITTED,

TO the jail of Loudoun county, as a runaway, on the 2d inst. a negro man, who calls himself

ELIAS DOWLING.

He is supposed to be 25 years of age, is about 6 feet high, not very black, has a scar on his forehead, and a blemish on the sight of his left eye. ---Says he belongs to Charles Dickinson, of Louisa county, Va. and has been hired to William Boxler, on the Chesapeake and Ohio Canal.

The owner of said negro is requested to come forward, prove property, pay charges, and take him away, otherwise he will be disposed of according to law.

EDWARD HAMMETT,
Jailor Loudoun co.

June 5, 1830.---22 tf

A newspaper clipping seeing the capture of an escaped slave who worked on the C&O Canal. Photo courtesy of Whilbr.org.

Historian Timothy Snyder looked at runaway slave advertisements that ran in newspapers while the canal was being built. He found twenty-seven advertisements that ran from 1829-1839. "In the case of twelve runaways, it is explicitly written that the escapees had at one time been, or were actively engaged in, working on the canal," Snyder wrote in his article, "The Chesapeake & Ohio Canal and the Underground Railroad."

While there was some slave labor involved in the construction of the canal, it wasn't the preferred method. Around the time, the Canal Company had decided to use indentured servants, the board of directors also passed a resolution to purchase 100 slaves. They never acted on this, according to Walter Sanderlin in *The Great National Project*. Similarly, when a chance to purchase 350 slaves came up in June of 1830, the board passed. The canal company had learned its lessons in trying to procure cheap labor.

"Therefore, any slaves who worked on the waterway must have been hired out by their owners to contractors that the company engaged to do work on the canal. Based on the runaway slaves ads, it can be concluded that the canal company utilized slave labor indirectly by hiring contractors who employed slaves," Snyder wrote.

Freed blacks did work on the canal as boatmen, mule walkers, and for a time as captains. The Journey Through Hallowed Ground website says that their numbers declined during the early 1800s. "The Virginia legislature, responding to slaveholder's fears that black boatmen assisted fugitive slaves, passed laws in the early-to-mid nineteenth century that mandated white supervision," according to Hallowedground.org.

Actions like this, as well as complaints from white boatmen, caused the C&O Canal Company to ban African Americans from captaining boats in 1856. Beginning the following year, all canal boats had to have at least one adult white person on board who was considered the "master" of the boat.

"The regulation banning black captains was never overturned. Even if it wasn't enforced after the Civil War, it did seem to have a dampening effect. After 1856 there were no black barge captions until 1878, when four men registered. Louis Roberson, Wilson Middleton, Kirk Fields, and J.M. Johnson all captained barges owned by three different coal companies," according to Hallowedground.org.

The regulations also did not stop escaping slaves from using the waterway. In fact, slaves escaping north most likely crossed the canal, such as James Curry. He wrote in *Narrative of James Curry, A Fugitive Slave*, "I then took the Montgomery road, but, wishing to escape Baltimore, I turned off, and it being cloudy, I lost my course, and fell back again upon the Potomac river, and travelled on the tow path of the canal from Friday night until Sunday morning, when I lay down and slept a little, and then, having no place to hide for the day, I determined to go on until I could find a place of safety."

Rumors persist that the canal was used as part of the Underground Railroad to transport escaping slaves, although no hard evidence such as journal or oral history exists to support it. There are cases where slaver owners believed that their slaves escaped on canal boats, though. In one such instance in 1869, William H. Benson in Montgomery County, Md., wrote about his escaped slave, Rufus Jackson, saying, "I have every reason to believe that he is making his way off on a canal boat."

Snyder wrote that no evidence could be found that that these instances were part of the organized effort of the Underground Railroad, though.

The Engineering Marvel Hidden Under a Mountain

On the day that construction began on the Chesapeake and Ohio Canal on July 4, 1828, the pressure was on the work crews to get dig the 184.5-mile-long ditch to Cumberland as quickly as possible.

Why the rush? The Baltimore and Ohio Railroad broke ground in Baltimore for its construction on the same day and Cumberland with its coal mines and agricultural products was the prize for both the canal and railroad. The first one to reach the city would be able to secure customers without competition until the other mode of transportation arrived.

The C&O Canal crews worked hard digging the canal and building 160 culverts, seventy-four lift locks and eleven aqueducts. However, the canal has only one tunnel—the Paw Paw Tunnel—and it was a major reason why the B&O Railroad beat the C&O Canal to Cumberland by eight years.

Construction

When planning the route of the C&O Canal, it could have continued to follow the Potomac River through southeastern Allegany County, weaving along the Paw Paw Bends or cut through a mountain. Following the bends in the river would have been the easier course, but cutting a tunnel through the mountain would save five miles and could be done in two years, according to the engineering estimates.

The C&O Canal Company chose the quicker route.

The contractor chosen to build the tunnel was a former Methodist minister named Lee Montgomery. He began hiring men to work on the tunnel in June 1836. The crews worked from either end of the tunnel digging into the mountain and from above cutting down into the mountain.

Workers sank four shafts into the mountain to work from above the mountain. The shafts were set in pairs; one shaft of each pair allowed for debris removal and the other was for ventilation. The northernmost pair of shafts was 122 feet deep and the southernmost pair of shafts was 188 feet deep.

One of the portals of the Paw Paw Tunnel, which was supposed to save the C&O Canal time in its race to Cumberland, Md. Photo courtesy of National Park Service.

The crews initially blasted away large areas of rock with black powder and then shaped the tunnel with picks and shovels. The rubble was hauled out of the tunnel with horse carts.

"The workers were not experts at blasting, and there was a great deal of overbreakage; the excavation was 40 percent larger than needed," Elizabeth Kytle wrote in *Home on the Canal*.

Once excavated, the tunnel arch was formed from layer upon layer of bricks. According to Kytle, the Paw Paw Tunnel lining is 13 layers of brick deep with some places having up to 33 layers. Any open spaces remaining above the arch were backfilled with the excavated material.

"The slaty rock was reasonably hard, but loose enough to make frequent trouble by caving in. It was dangerous work and it went at a snail's pace," Kytle wrote.

Montgomery had projected before construction began that his crews would be able to bore out seven to eight feet a day. The reality turned out to be that his crews working three shifts each day only managed 10 to 12 feet a week.

To complicate matters, work was suspended on the tunnel from 1842 to 1847 because of the C&O Canal Company's financial problems. Construction didn't resume until November 1848. It was completed by a different contractor, McCulloh and Day, and opened for navigation on October 10, 1850.

The final 3,118-foot-long tunnel is called "the greatest single engineering achievement on the canal," by the National Park Service. It is 22 feet wide and 24 feet wide and sheathed in more than 11 million bricks.

Operation

Though the Paw Paw tunnel was an engineering marvel, it was narrow for purposes of the canal. The canal was designed so that boats could pass each other going in opposite directions. The towpath and canal bed through the Paw Paw Tunnel were both only wide enough for one set of canal mules and one canal boat to move through the tunnel.

Because of the length of the tunnel, a canaller upon reaching one entrance of the tunnel could tell if another boat was already in the tunnel (if it was daylight), but it was impossible to tell if the boat was approaching or heading away. The canallers started lighting colored lanterns fore and aft on their boats to distinguish direction. A green lantern was hung fore and a red lantern was hung aft. That way, other canallers could tell whether boats in the tunnel were coming or going.

If the boat was showing a green light, the canal boat captain knew that the boat was approaching and pulled over to wait.

Not that problems still didn't arise.

Leaving the Paw Paw Tunnel at its eastern end. Photo courtesy of the National Park Service.

Some canal boat captains who were in a rush or just plain cranky, refused to yield the right of way to boats in the tunnel. George Hooper Wolfe tells one of the stories in his book

I Drove Mules on the C&O Canal.

Two captains—Jim McAlvey and Cletus Zimmerman—and their boats met in the middle of the tunnel. Neither man wanted to back up, and the captains got into a fist fight over who had the right of way. Then things escalated.

"A gun was drawn and would have been used but for the quick action of a mule driver who knocked the gun from the captain's hand into the Canal," Wolfe wrote.

Other boats began entering the canal from both ends of the tunnel and soon the tunnel was filled with boats. As day gave way to evening, crew members on the unmoving boats started corn cob fires in their cabin stoves to cook meals. Before too long, the tunnel began filling with smoke from the stoves and made staying in the tunnel very uncomfortable.

This sped up negotiations and the captains reached an agreement so that the boats could start moving again.

When traffic on the canal reached its peak during the 1870's, a watchman was hired to help regulate the traffic at the Paw Paw Tunnel and keep it from becoming a bottleneck. The watchman enforced the canal company rules for using the tunnel and could fine canal boat captains $10 for violating them.

The Tunnel Today

Even today, the Paw Paw Tunnel is still an impressive structure on the C&O Canal and it is still isolated. While there is a parking area just off Route 51 between Paw Paw, W.Va., and Oldtown, Md., visitors still have to walk about half a mile along the towpath to reach the tunnel.

A flashlight is recommended if you want to walk through the tunnel since it is quite dark and there is no interior lighting. It will also allow you to see some of the features of the tunnel, including the weep holes (openings in the brick liner that allow water to pass through), the rope burns on the wooden railing and the brass plates the serve as 100-foot markers inside the tunnel.

Healthy and energetic visitors can also hike a steep two-mile long, Tunnel Hill Trail, over the mountain. This trail passes by where the canal builders lived while the tunnel was being built.

Expanding the C&O Canal

Before the Chesapeake & Ohio Canal was even complete, thought was being given to how to expand its reach. "At one time or another almost every major tributary of the Potomac was considered as the site of a possible feeder," Walter S. Sanderlin wrote in *The Great National Project*. Three ideas showed merit and were actually given serious consideration. Two were actually built.

The Washington City Canal

The Washington City Canal actually started operating before the C&O Canal even broke ground. It was a short canal of 2.25 miles. It passed through Washington City connected the Anacostia River with the Potomac River and Tiber Creek.

When discussions to build the canal began, the idea was to connect the navigable Anacostia River with the Potomac River, which George Washington's Patowmack Company had made passable. Pierre Charles L'Enfant, the man who designed Washington City, supported the construction of such a canal.

A 1796 private lottery to raise funds for the construction failed. This curtailed the work that was done until 1802. That is when Congress granted the Washington Canal a charter. This spurred development for a short time, but funding was still lacking.

In 1809, Congress created a new canal company and capitalized it with $100,000. The new company broke ground on May 2, 1810, with a ceremony at the present-day intersection of New Jersey Avenue and E St. SE that President James Madison attended. The War of 1812 delayed the construction, but the Washington City Canal finally opened on November 21, 1815.

A bird's-eye view of Washington in the 1800s, showing the Washington City Canal. Photo courtesy of the Library of Congress.

The canal began at the Anacostia River near the Washington Navy Yard and moved north and northwest. Another branch ran north and northeast from James Creek. The two branches converged and ran north toward the Capitol Building. It moved northwest at the base of Capitol Hill and then moved north across what is now the National Mall. Then it turned west until it joined Tiber Creek and eventually the Potomac River.

One of the problems with the Washington City Canal was that it could only accommodate boats that drew three feet or less. Also, it could not handle the Anacostia River's tidal shifts. Sometimes, it overflowed its banks. At other times, the water was too shallow to navigate. The tidal variations also left sediment deposited in the canal that reduced its depth.

Washington City bought the company in 1831 and tried to make repairs. Congress allocated funds for repairs in 1833. This allowed for the connection to the under-construction C&O Canal to be made. It became known as the C&O Canal Washington Branch.

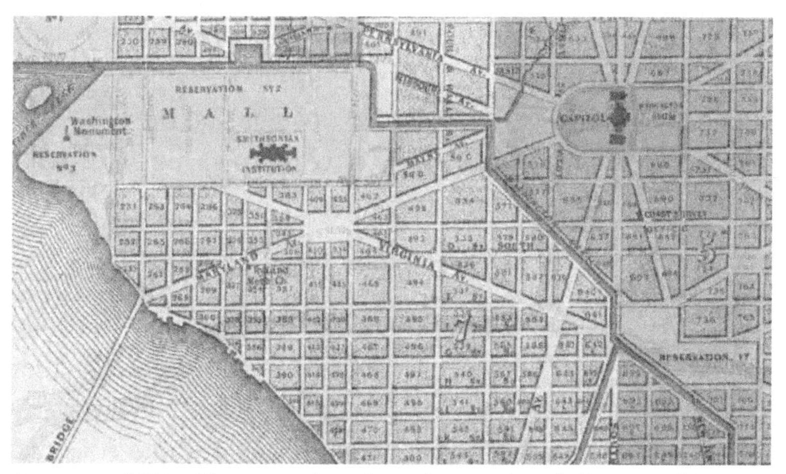

A map of Washington showing the path of the Washington City Canal through the city. Courtesy of Wikimedia Commons.

"The organization of the Chesapeake and Ohio Canal Company revived interest in the city canal as a means by which the trade of the former could be brought into Washington," Sanderlin wrote.

A lockkeeper's house was built at the southwest corner of Constitution Ave. NW and 17th Street NW for a canal employee to live and manage traffic between the two canals. The house can still be seen at the site, although the canal has long since been filled in.

Congress allocated money to deepen the Washington

Branch in 1849, but Washington City was required to provide matching funds, which caused problems. Also, contractor problems slowed down the improvements so that they weren't completed until the 1850s.

By this time, the peak years of canals in America had passed, and there was more interest in building railroads. Traffic on the extension continued to decline until, by the Civil War, the extension was used as a sewer and storm drain for the city.

Residents complained about the disease and smell associated with the canal, and by 1871, officials started to fill in sections of the canal. Constitution Avenue and the northwest portion of Washington Avenue now run over much of what was once the Washington Extension.

The Alexandria Canal

When the construction of the C&O Canal was announced, merchants in Alexandria were excited because they believed it would be an economic boon for them. On November 10, 1827, they subscribed $250,000 to the construction of the canal with the option to build their own canal that connected to it.

Once the merchants saw that most of the canal business was staying in Georgetown and Washington, they exercised their option to build their connecting canal in 1830. Because the city was within the boundary of the District of Columbia, Congress had to grant the charter to form a canal company, which it did. The government also allocated $400,000 for its construction.

The groundbreaking ceremony took place on July 4, 1831, three years to the day of the C&O Canal's groundbreaking. Work on the canal began July 9.

The most-significant challenge facing the Alexandria Canal Company was how to get the canal boats from the C&O Canal across the Potomac River to Virginia. One rejected idea was to build a dam across the Potomac to create a slackwater area so that canal boats could be towed across the river.

The remnants of one the Alexandria Canal's aqueducts in Alexandria, Va. Photo courtesy of Wikimedia Commons.

The Alexandria Canal Company decided instead to build an aqueduct across the river that would connect the two canals.

"The 'Potomac Aqueduct' was to become the most expensive item on the 7.25-mile long canal, costing approximately $600,000 instead of the $202,552, estimate, or nearly one-half of the cost of the $1,250,000 required to complete the canal," Thomas Swiftwater Hahn and Emory L. Kemp wrote in *The Alexandria Canal: Its History & Preservation.*

Construction on the aqueduct began in 1832, and it was the last piece of the canal to be finished in 1843 when the Alexandria Canal started to operate.

Wharfs on the Alexandria Canal. Photo courtesy of Wikimedia Commons.

The completed aqueduct has six stone piers and two abutments, each of which is 21 feet thick at the high-water mark. "Each of the piers had a timber ice-breaker on the upstream side, shaped like an oblique cone pointing upstream," Hahn and Kemp wrote.

Like the Paw Paw Tunnel and the Georgetown Incline Plane would be upon their completion, the Potomac Aqueduct was considered the engineering marvel of its time.

The *Alexandria Gazette* announced that the watering of the new canal would happen on July 4, 1843:

"The water is to be let into this magnificent work, but which the connexion between Alexandria and the Chesapeake and Ohio Canal is established, on Tuesday, the Fourth of July. … The work now stands as a monument of the proficiency of the present age of Engineering. As a hydraulic work, it ranks number one, and may be boldly pointed to in comparison with any thin at home or abroad."

The newspaper jumped the gun with the announcement, however. The actual watering didn't happen until July 6. Then the following day part of the towpath and protective wall on the causeway settled and gave way. The canal needed to be drained to prevent a breach.

A canal boat leaves the C&O Canal and enters the Potomac Aqueduct to pass over the Potomac River to the Alexandria Canal. Photo courtesy of the National Park Service.

It was not until late November 1843 that the canal was repaired and opened for business. Once open, boats could pass from the C&O Canal onto the Alexandria Canal and travel just over seven miles to the tidal lock in Alexandria.

Before the opening of the C&O Canal at Cumberland, Md., Alexandria received primarily agricultural product and sent primarily manufactured goods and fish on the canal, according to Hahn and Kemp. After 1850, the wharves at Alexandria started receiving more and more coal.

The Alexandria Canal may have been short, but it tended

to get damaged every time the Potomac River flooded, which made it expensive to maintain. Those same floods also interrupted traffic on the canal and a reduction of tolls.

"It was not surprising, then, to learn that on 1 May 1859, only 48 cents remained in the treasury of the Alexandria Canal Company!" Hahn and Kemp wrote.

Once the Civil War started, Federal troops occupied the Virginia side of the aqueduct to ensure its use for troop transport. Since the towpath was too narrow to move equipment efficiently, the aqueduct was drained in 1861, and the floor of the aqueduct was covered with four-inch-thick planks to create a wagon road into Virginia.

After the war, there was interest in reviving the canal, but Alexandria and Virginia couldn't afford to pay for the repairs needed to make it operational again. The Virginia Assembly passed an act requiring the city to divest itself of the canal stock.

The city fathers made a deal with the Alexandria Railroad and Bridge Company to lease them the canal for ninety-nine years at $1,000 a year if they would operate and maintain the canal.

In 1867, the company built a highway toll bridge above the aqueduct for other types of traffic to cross the river.

By the mid-1870s, the coal trade on the canal began to decrease, and the Alexandria Canal was abandoned by 1886. The canal bed and towpath were still useful, though. Part of it became an Arlington, Va., trolley line in 1896. It traveled along the canal's west side. That same year, another portion was used for part of the line of the Washington Southern Railway. From Arlington National Cemetery to the Potomac River, the rail line traveled along the former canal route.

When the Key Bridge was built in 1923, the old aqueduct was removed, leaving only the abutments. Also, when the area around the tidal basin was developed, the old basin and tidal lock were incorporated into the landscaping.

The Baltimore Cross-Cut Canal

Baltimore, Md., and the state of Maryland had wanted a canal built from the city to the C&O Canal even before construction began on the C&O Canal. That interest continued during construction, although the Baltimore and Ohio Railroad was being built accomplish the same purpose as a canal from Baltimore.

Three surveys were made in March 1837 to try and find a possible way to link the C&O Canal to Baltimore. The Maryland Canal Company was even created to manage this extension.

The legal fighting with the Baltimore and Ohio Railroad at Point of Rocks and the federal government's decision to pull back its support had left the Canal Company in need of cash to continue construction. The directors sought the help of the Maryland Legislature.

The legislature agreed to provide funding, but with conditions. It passed a resolution that read, in part, "That the Maryland Canal Company are entitled to no subscription on the part of this State, under the provisions of this act of the assembly, unless they will agree to locate the canal from the Chesapeake and Ohio Canal to the city of Baltimore by the most northern practicable rout the of the routes by the valleys of the Monocacy and the Patapsco, or by a route diverging from the said Chesapeake and Ohio Canal at the mouth of the Seneca River, exclusively within the limits of the State, provided such route be found practicable, with due supply of water."

Three routes called the Westminster, the Monocacy-Linganore, and the Seneca routes were surveyed. All three were found impracticable because of an insufficient supply of water on the summit level, according to Canal Historian Harlan Unrau in *Historic Resource Study: Chesapeake & Ohio Canal.*

The only feasible way the engineers saw was not to run a canal across the state but to bring the goods into Georgetown and then use the Anacostia River to reach Baltimore.

"In finding no feasible direct connections between Baltimore and the Potomac valley, the engineers studying the Maryland Cross-Cut Canal never investigated innovative approaches, such as the use of inclined planes as was being used on the Morris Canal in New Jersey," Robert J. Kapsch wrote in his paper, "Baltimore and the Maryland Cross-Cut Canal: 1820-1851."

An 1838 report by Col. J.J. Abert with the U.S. Engineering Department, confirmed the finding of the original survey. However, Abert wrote that he had found a fourth route from the Seneca River to the Patapsco River via Brookeville. This was studied further, and the estimated construction cost came in at $11.6 million or more than twice as much as the estimate for building the C&O Canal. This exorbitant price tag killed talk of the canal for a while.

It was revived again when the C&O Canal opened to Cumberland. This time, it was found to be too expensive to build while at the same time, the railroad was living up to its promise and had already pushed further westward.

"The Maryland Cross-Cut canal became the most studied canal never to be constructed in the U.S.," Kapsch wrote.

The Canal Snags on Point of Rocks

The Chesapeake and Ohio Canal was a construction and engineering challenge for its time. The canal's charter required that 100 operable miles be built within five years. Benjamin Wright who had overseen the construction of the Erie Canal was chosen for the same job on the C&O Canal.

The canal construction involved more than just digging a trench across the level land and making it watertight. Boats traveling from Georgetown in the District of Columbia to Cumberland, Md., had to be lifted more than 600 feet on their westward journey. Rivers needed to be crossed and mountains gone over, around, or through.

The 184.5-mile-long C&O Canal was built in sections bid out to independent contractors. The laborers were mainly imported Irishman, who jumped at the chance to come to America, though they quickly found the work unsatisfying. The work was hard, and the tools were picks, shovels, horses and black powder.

The canal hits its first major snag at Point of Rocks in Frederick County, Md.

The canal was watered by dams built on the Potomac River. As the canal construction reached one of the barriers, water impounded by the dam was allowed to flow into the completed portion of the canal. The first dam was at Little Falls. When the canal reached that point, that first section of the canal was placed into operation.

This happened in November 1830, almost two and a half years after the canal's groundbreaking ceremony. It allowed the first five miles of the canal to be used.

The following summer, construction reached the second dam at Seneca and opened the first 22 miles of the canal to navigations.

At Point of Rocks, there was room for either the railroad or the canal. The legal challenges over the land nearly doomed the canal. Photo courtesy of the National Park Service.

The third dam was near Harpers Ferry. Reaching this barrier would have opened up 62 miles of canal, but to get from Seneca to Harpers Ferry, the canal would have to pass through a narrow area of land called Point of Rocks, and that's where the forward progress of the canal stopped.

It was believed that the land there was wide enough for

either the canal or the Baltimore and Ohio Railroad.

The B&O Railroad claimed the right of way through Point of Rocks. The C&O Canal Company thought it had the right of way through Point of Rocks by its own charter and the charter of the Patowmack Company, which it had taken over.

The canal has just assumed its rights were secure, but the railroad company was aggressively trying to secure its claim to the area, including getting waivers from landowners in the area, including Charles Carroll. He was a supporter of the railroad and a landowner in the area, and he fought the C&O Canal Company's right of way and encouraged other landowners to follow suit.

The case went to court and stayed there four years, during which the C&O Canal could make no progress. Even if it had continued construction on the other side of Point of Rocks and reached the dam near Harpers Ferry, it would have been watering a canal to nowhere.

Meanwhile, construction on the railroad continued.

The case was eventually decided in favor of the C&O Canal, but it left the company a financial wreck. The federal government with a new administration had grown disillusioned with the idea of the canal and stopped supporting it.

The canal company found new funding from the State of Maryland, but only after promising to build a canal extension to Baltimore if it was feasible.

While the court decided in favor of the canal, it did allow the railroad to also build through Point of Rocks afterward if there was room. Although there was space for a single line through the area, when a second rail line was laid years later, a tunnel had to be built through Catoctin Mountain.

This meant that the canal and railroad were running side by side though Point of Rocks. This would happen at a couple other areas along the canal. These locations allowed for some venting of frustration between canallers and railroaders. The train engineers would show their animosity toward the canal by blowing their whistles when they passed canal boats in the hopes of startling the mules.

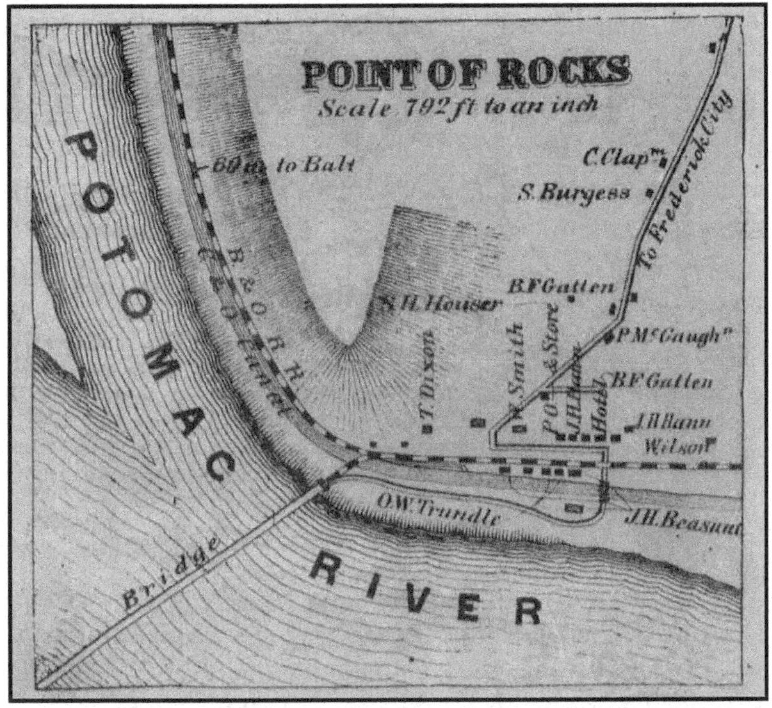

A map of Point of Rocks showing the canal and railroad running side by side. Photo courtesy of Wikimedia Commons.

Locks and Lockhouses

When the brass horn would sound at all hours, day and night, the lockkeepers of the Chesapeake and Ohio Canal would leave what they were doing and head for their locks. No matter the weather outside, their job was to set the lock for the approaching canal boats.

Each lock would lift or lower a canal boat around ten feet as the canallers hauled coal and other cargo down the Appalachian Mountains from Cumberland, Md. to Georgetown and back.

Nowadays, most of the canal is just an empty ditch, but many of the canal houses remain. Carol Patch of Arlington, Va., hosts an evening dinner party at Lockhouse 10 once a year for her friends. It is one of six lockhouses available for rent along the C&O Canal.

Lockhouse 10 is decorated as it would have been in the 1930s so it has electricity and indoor plumbing. However, the kitchen equipment certainly doesn't include a microwave and dishwasher.

"It reminds us of how hard our mothers had it," Patch said.

A Lockkeeper's Life

A C&O Canal lockkeeper had to be on the job whenever the canal was open, an average of ten months a year. For this, they were paid a small salary based on the number of locks they tended, given a plot of ground on which they could plant a garden, and a lockhouse in which to live.

When the canal was closed during the winter, lockkeepers only received half pay. They could make up the difference by repairing the drained canal or doing other work for the company.

Married men were preferred over bachelors because with children, married lockkeepers had more help. For a time, there were even female lockkeepers, usually the widows of lockkeepers. However, the C&O Canal Company decided to discharge any by 1835 to increase efficiency. This wasn't a reflection on their work so much as their strength. It was physically taxing to lock a boat through and it was believed to the work was better suited for men.

A canal boat passes through one of the seventy-four locks along the C&O Canal. Photo courtesy of the National Park Service.

Locking Through

The C&O Canal has seventy-four locks that raise and lower boats. As a canal boat approached a lock, the canaller would call out "Heeeeeey, lock!" or blow a horn. The lock-keeper would come out and make sure that the lock gates were open for the incoming boat.

For instance, if the boat was moving downriver, the mules would pull the boat as the captain steered it into the lock. Ropes were tossed ashore and wrapped around snubbing posts (thick logs set in the ground). The slack was taken up on the ropes to act as a brake on the canal boat to keep it from crashing into the opposite set of lock gates, which were closed.

The locks were built barely large enough to contain the ninety-two-foot-long and fourteen-foot-wide canal boats. Once the boat was stopped inside the lock, the lock gates behind the canal boat were closed.

Lock gates were designed so that they formed a point upriver when closed. In this way, water flowing against the gates helped keep them closed and sealed. Sluice valves at the bottom of the downriver lock gates were then opened with large rod-like keys. Water from inside the lock flowed out of the lock through the sluice valves. Since the upriver gates were closed, the water level inside the lock quickly fell.

As the boat was lowered, the ropes around the snubbing posts were gradually let out. By maintaining tension on the ropes, the boat could be stabilized somewhat so that it wouldn't bounce around inside the lock and either damage the lock or the boat.

When the level inside the lock matched that outside of the downriver lock gates, the sluice gates were closed and the downriver lock gates opened. The mules pulled the boat out of the lock to continue it journey downriver.

The entire process of locking through took about fifteen minutes, although some records indicate that it could be routinely done under ten minutes.

One of the seventy-six lockhouses built for C&O Canal lockkeepers so they could be near their work. Photo courtesy of the National Park Service.

Lockhouses

The lockhouses on the lower end of the canal were originally built from stone, but good quality stone became harder to find and the financial pinch started to be felt so that after mile 24, other materials were introduced including brick, wood frame and logs.

The basic design of a lockhouse was generally 18x30 feet and two floors. The biggest difference, besides, materials, at the time they were built was whether they had a basement and the placement of the chimney.

The first lockhouses were built on contract and cost $725

each. The first floor has two rooms, a kitchen and a parlor. The upstairs also had two room with only three feet of clearance at the eaves.

Some of them were enlarged. The most notable was the Great Falls Tavern, which the canal company authorized to be enlarged in order to capture the tourist trade coming to the Great Falls. Crommelin, Md., and Rushville, Md., had taverns in their lockhouses. While drinking was prohibited on the canal, it was a directive that many lockkeepers chose to ignore. Not only did the lockkeepers drink, but they often sold liquor to canallers.

While a drunken canaller could crash his boat, drunken lockkeepers could be just as dangerous. In one instance, the canal boat *Exselsior* was locking through, when a drunk lockkeeper opened the paddles on the lower doors before the boat was fully in the lock, despite the warning of the boat captain. The water started falling and the boat caught on the sill and wound up breaking in half. It caused $1,300 in damage and a lot of lost time for canal boats that couldn't continue the trip on the canal.

Of better use for the canal was when the lockkeeper opened a store in his house so sell provisions to canallers. These could also be separate businesses set up along the canal with the permission of the company.

Canal Quarters Program

Of the seventy-six lockhouses built to help run the C&O Canal, only twenty remain. Of those twenty, six can be rented for a night as part of the C&O Canal Trust's Canal Quarters Program.

"It's a partnership between the C&O Canal Trust and the National Historic Park," said Heidi Schlag, director of communications for the C&O Canal Trust. "The park was looking for a way to preserve the lockhouses and we were looking for a way to help the park."

The program began in 2009 when the Canal Trust and National Park Service restored three different lockhouses to different periods of time along the canal. Some had amenities. Some were considered rustic.

"Lockhouses 6 and 10 are the ones with amenities and they are very popular," Schlag said. "You usually have to book them six months in advance."

The lockhouses with amenities have heat, air conditioning, electricity and running water. People who stay in the rustic lockhouses have to use a porta-john for a bathroom and an outdoor hand pump for water. It may seem odd that someone would want to stay in such a place, but it gives the guests an idea of what life was like for a lockkeeper and his family during the particular time period to which that lockhouse has been restored.

Visitors can also find interpretive information, such as panels and scrapbooks, in the lockhouse that explain what was happening on the canal during the particular time to which the house has been restored. Stonebraker likes to read the stories collected in the scrapbooks, many of which feature people who used to live in that particular lockhouse.

Celebrating the Opening of the C&O Canal

October 9, 1850, "dawned upon the mountains in all the richness of the early autumn...," according to the *Cumberland Civilian.* People were always on the move with early morning chores, trying to squeeze the most from the diminishing daylight hours. On this Thursday, large crowds began gathering in front of the United States Hotel and Barnum House in Cumberland, Md.

Many in the crowds were special guests from Maryland, Virginia, the District of Columbia, and the towns and counties along the route of the Chesapeake and Ohio Canal. They were in Cumberland for the opening of the canal's eastern section. They had arrived in the city the day before, and ironically, they had come on the Baltimore and Ohio Railroad, the canal's greatest competitor. Although the canal and railroad had both broken ground on July 4, 1828, the railroad had reached Cumberland eight years earlier.

The Independent Blues of Baltimore played a selection of songs for the crowd that "electrified an immense multitude of our citizens with their unsurpassed instrumental performance," according to the *Civilian.*

Another invited group was the Eckhart Artillery, which performed "various military evolutions in a manner that would have done credit to a veteran corps," according to the newspaper.

Around 9 a.m., a procession led by Col. Pickell of Baltimore formed and headed toward the canal outlet locks.

"On arriving at this point, and after the firing of a salute by the Artillerists, William Price, Esq. on behalf of the corporate authorities and citizens, in a neat speech, welcomed the Canal Board and their guests, and congratulated them upon the occurrence of the event so long looked for - the opening of the Canal to Cumberland," the *Baltimore Sun* reported.

Gen. James M. Coale, the president of the C&O Canal Company, spoke next briefly reviewing the history and progress of canal. He also pointed out that Cumberland was just the completion of the eastern portion of the canal. The western portion was still planned to connect tidewater with the Ohio River and points west.

The outlet locks were opened as boats began to enter the canal. Members of the C&O Canal board and their guests boarded the *Jenny Lind.* The Independent Blues and other special guests boarded the *Charles B. Fisk.* Two other excursion boats were crowded with the Eckhart Artillery, Mechanic's Band of Cumberland, and other citizens.

These boats started down the canal around 11 p.m. The bands provided music for the trip. The passenger boats were followed by five canal boats – *Southampton, Elizabeth, Ohio, Delaware,* and *Freeman Rawdon* – loaded with coal.

The passenger boats stopped about 10 miles down the canal where the guests enjoyed a banquet of fine wine and delicious food on board the *Charles B. Fisk.* Meanwhile, the loaded canal boats continued eastward.

They returned to Cumberland around 8 p.m. The citizens of Cumberland hosted the group for another banquet and a ball at Heflefinger's Hotel.

"After twenty-two years of intermittent enthusiasm and despair, the Chesapeake and Ohio Canal was completed to

Cumberland," Walter Sanderlin wrote in *The Great National Project.*

In its final year of construction, many might have wondered if it would be completed. The board had been forced to economize on some materials. Laborers who had been unpaid for a while stopped working in April had caused a work suspension on the canal. The date for the opening, which had originally been set for July 1, was pushed back multiple times.

As for the loaded boats, one went as far as Williamsport, Md. Two of the boats got stuck above Dam No. 5 because of low water in the canal and they were drawing too much water. This left the *Freeman Rawdon* and *Southampton* competing to be the first boat to complete the eastern section of the C&O Canal.

"Horses and mules were requisitioned along the way to maintain the speed, and the boats arrived within a short time of each other," Sanderlin wrote.

The *Freeman Rawdon* was the first boat to Georgetown, reaching the tidal lock around 6 p.m. on October 17, 1850.

The War Between the States

The Real Mason Dixon Line

The Mason Dixon line surveyed by Charles Mason and Jeremiah Dixon between 1763 and 1767 resolved a border dispute between Maryland, Pennsylvania, and Delaware. Over the years, it also came to represent the unofficial border between the northern and southern states.

However, while Maryland leaned heavily towards the Confederate States in its sympathies, it remained in the Union during the Civil War. This meant that the border between the Union and Confederacy in the east was the Potomac River.

Canallers who traveled along the northern shore of the Potomac River on the Chesapeake and Ohio Canal were often caught in the crossfire between two nations … literally.

C&O Canal Company was optimistic about the 1861 boating season. Finances for the company were still rough, but repairs had been made over the winter and even the long-delayed work on Dam 4 was completed. The *Williamsport Ledger* reported, "so long looked for, so long deferred, will, we have no doubt, be received by all parties interested in the welfare of the canal with feelings of unmingled joy."

The Western Maryland coal companies were happy that a tariff had been passed on foreign coal. This meant that demand had increased for domestic coal.

The C&O Canal opened for the season in the middle of March and went along well for a while. In April, heavy rains started along the canal. The Potomac rose and fell and then rose again washing over the towpath and causing two breaks—one at Seneca, Md., and one at Williamsport, Md.

Travel on the canal was suspended for a month while repairs began. This happened right about the same time that the break in the country began, and the Civil War started.

Confederate raiders create a breach in the canal to disrupt the transportation route. Photo courtesy of Sonofthesouth.net.

In the first three months of the war, traffic on the canal fell off sharply. Boaters were nervous. The Union government had troops marching on the towpath. Confederate raiders were raiding boats and destroying locks.

In May 1861, the company collected only four percent of the tolls that it collected in two weeks of boating in March. In June, it barely collected one percent of the tolls.

On June 26, Andrew K. Stake, the canal company's general superintendent, wrote, "Nothing but soldiers, baggage, wagons, camps, guns, pistols and swords meets our gaze here, wherever we go. They have pretty nearly eaten up everything we have. I hope they will get away soon."

While food supplies were an attractive target in order to help feed an army, coal was also a potential target.. It worked well in helping run steamships and smelting furnaces. Shutting down the canal would not only make the Washington politicians uncomfortable in the winter, but it would slow down iron production and steamship travel.

Canal boats were considered military targets and Confederate soldiers made a habit of commandeering them at the start of the war and confiscating their cargo. If they could not steal the cargo, the Confederates could burn the canal boats while they were in the canal. Not only would it destroy the coal in the burned boat, it would delay traffic on the canal for days while the wreckage of the burned boats was removed.

Thomas McKaig

The first instance of this was in April 1861. Charles Wenner was a grain merchant who lived in Berlin. He owned a warehouse and two canal boats, which he used to carry his grain to Georgetown where it could be sold. On April 24, 1861, he had one of his boats loaded up and ready to head down the canal. A group of horsemen from Virginia rode up and demanded that he surrender the boat by the authority of the commanding officer at Harpers Ferry. The men took command of the boat and moved it downriver to Point of Rocks, Md. There they unloaded the boat and sent the cargo in wagons over the bridge into Virginia.

In another instance, a boat owned by Thomas McKaig, a

state legislator, was held at Harpers Ferry until all the salt it was carrying in its holds was removed.

In most instances, this would be called piracy, but McKaig was a Southern sympathizer. Historians still debate whether he might have made arrangements to deliver the salt to the Confederacy rather than the Union.

The most likely places for piracy to happen were near the points on the canal where it actually opened into the Potomac River. This was Big Slackwater at Dam No. 4 and Little Slackwater at Dam No. 5. Though the river was usually unreliable for navigation, water backed up enough behind these dams to create a reliably deep area for canal boats to navigate. It also provided an area where a pirated boat could be taken into the river and over to Virginia.

The Civil War helped the canal in one way. The B&O Railroad had weaknesses that the south exploited. In areas where the railroad passed through Virginia, Confederate soldiers stopped passage of trains. In the north, sympathizers burned railroad bridges and tore up rails. It was a lot easier, it seems, to destroy the railroad than to destroy the canal.

The canal had an aqueduct that transported boats over the Potomac River to Alexandria, Va., so the wharfs at Georgetown could get some relief from the incoming traffic. It also helped out the wharf owners in Alexandria who could get some of the canal trade. This was fine when the states were united, but when the war started, canal boats couldn't be allowed to pass into enemy territory.

The Union Army took over the aqueduct, closed it off, and drained it. Then because they feared the drained aqueduct could represent a roadway from Virginia right into Washington, they posted guards on the aqueduct.

The uncertainty of who was friend or foe became part of canal life during the Civil War.

From Building Boats to Healing Soldiers

It's uncertain who pleaded with the Sisters of Charity of Cincinnati to care for the thousands of wounded soldiers in Cumberland, Md, at the start of the Civil War. At least three people are credited with making the case for the sisters' help in the city. What is certain is that the sisters responded quickly to the call for aid.

"On the 16th of February 1861 – there came a hasty call for Sisters of Charity to go to Cumberland, Md. to nurse the sick and wounded soldiers. ...I had just a half hour to prepare for the journey," Sister Gabriella Crowe wrote.

Though Cumberland was far from much of the fighting during the Civil War, the city sat along the Baltimore and Ohio Railroad line, at the end of the C&O Canal, and at the beginning of the National Road. This made it easy for wounded sent to Cumberland or other cities along the transportation routes. Though the soldiers could receive better care at a hospital behind the lines, many of them were too injured or sick to survive the bumpy, crowded ride to the hospital. Those that did were much worse for wear when they arrived at Cumberland.

In less than a year, the city quickly become a medical center where one out of four people were either sick or wounded.

Records show that the eight Catholic sisters, along with Mother Josephine Harvey and Father Edward Collins left on the B&O Railroad on the afternoon of February 15, 1861. In the rush to get to Cumberland, Dr. McMahon who was the sisters' escort on the trip missed the train. Sister Anthony O'Connell caught the train just in time and left on it thinking the other sisters had already boarded. They hadn't realized that they were still waiting for Dr. Mahon.

The Angels of the Battlefield painting shows Catholic sisters at work caring for the Civil War wounded. Photo courtesy of Sisters of Charity of Cincinnati.

Sis. Anthony got as far as Columbus, Ohio, when she received a telegram from from Archbishop John Purcell that read, "Return at once. Two boat loads of wounded soldiers from Pittsburg Landing, to be cared for!" Most likely, these were wounded from the fighting at Fort Donelson, which was going on in Tennessee at the time, which is where Pittsburg Landing was located.

With Sis. Anthony no longer part of the group, the remaining sisters, Dr. McMahon and Rev. Collins finally left for Cumberland around 8 p.m. They reached Wheeling, Va., (West Virginia would not become a state until the following year) at noon the next day. They stayed the night at the Visitation Convent there. They left the following morning on Feb. 17 "in a blinding snowstorm" and reached Cumberland in the evening.

Dr. George Suckley, the medical director in Cumberland, met the sisters at the train station and walked them downtown to a hotel that had been confiscated by Union army. Their appearance on the street drew a crowd of gawkers to whom Catholic sisters were an unfamiliar sight. At the hotel, the sisters took supper in the dining room.

Sister Ambrosia Schwartz

"While we were waiting for supper the windows were besieged without by children, white and black, peeping in to see the curiosity," wrote Sis. Gabriella Crowe.

With the shortage of rooms in the city, the Sisters of Charity slept their first night in Cumberland on the floor in a reception room of the hotel that was filled with soldiers.

Dr. McMahon took them on a tour of the hospital facilities in Cumberland the next day. Large buildings, including some of the warehouses along the Chesapeake and Ohio Canal, had been confiscated for use as hospitals.

Sister Gabriella Crowe

The hospitals had been set up so that the first floor was used for general purposes, such as housekeeping, cooking, storage, etc. while the upper floors had wards for the sick. On average, the hospitals held about fifty beds each, though they were often overcrowded after major battles. At the time, Cumberland had fourteen hospitals overcrowded with more than 2,200 sick soldiers.

Most of the patients at this time were suffering from typhoid, pneumonia, or erysipelas. According to *Baltimore Catholic Messenger*, the men were from Gen. Frederick Lander's division who had suffered from exposure while camped on the banks of Potomac and Patterson's Creek during the cold winter. Lander would die from his illness in March.

As the Sisters of Charity began assumed nursing duties in Cumberland, they quickly learned that the hospitals weren't that well supplied. They began making lists of what they would need to remedy that situation. The other problem they found was harder to deal with.

"The accommodations were poor, the weather cold, and the hospitals of which they were twelve, at some distance from one another, making it difficult, impossible for seven Sisters to give proper attention to the poor sufferers," Sis. Ambrosia Schwartz wrote.

This would have been especially true for the warehouses around the canal that were being used as hospitals. They offered plenty of room for wounded and sick, but they were also drafty.

After visiting each hospital building, the Sisters of Charity retired to find that a more-proper room had been found for them. Father Collins took them to the home of a Dr. Healy who was a Southern sympathizer. The doctor had fled Cumberland with the arrival of the Union army and had been commissioned a captain in the Confederate army. His wife, however, had remained behind.

Because of her husband's sympathies, the army had felt free to confiscate nearly all of the items in the house, leaving the woman so destitute that she needed to take in boarders to survive.

Sister Jane Garvin

"This lady manifested much kindness towards us, but this went no further than words as all her property had been confiscated, she was often obliged to accept our provisions to sustain life," Sis. Agnes Phillips wrote.

The sisters now had rooms, but their beds not much better than the floor of the hotel. The beds were rough boards covered with straw ticks and pillows stuffed with straw.

The sisters then settled in for what would be a three-month stay in Cumberland. The work would be challenging and never finished.

When the thousands of wounded and sick soldiers in Cumberland threatened to overload the city's ability to care for them, they called for help from the Sisters of Charity of Cincinnati. The sisters were one of the few groups in the country at the time that had any professional nursing experience and they were more than willing to help.

"We are delighted also at the arrival of the Sisters, chiefly at this time, when so many once robust and stout men, young and old, are now lying prostrate in hospitals in the midst of strangers, far from their home, dear friends and relations, but whose hearts will soon my gladdened and whose sad condition will soon be ameliorated by the constant, tender, and more than maternal care of the Sisters of Charity," one official wrote the Quartermaster General.

Besides working as nurses, the sisters also took on the duties of cooks, housekeepers and hospital administrators.

Sister Mary Agnes Phillips

"The sick men seem astonished and cannot comprehend the devotedness, the zeal and unwearying patience of the Sisters. Some declared that had the Sisters been here from the beginning, not a man would have died," the *Baltimore Mirror* reported.

Sis. Ambrosia Schwartz wrote that their duties were fatiguing and often disgusting because of the blood and wounds they had to deal with. However, due to the hard work and management of other workers by the Sisters of Charity, the hospitals soon became cleaner and the food better suited to something for wounded men to eat.

"One poor fellow said to me, Oh! Mother had you and your Sisters come sooner many of our poor boys would not be dead. He said no one could have any idea what they have suffered and endured for want of care and proper nursing. One poor fellow they say, a few hours before he died wrote on the wall by his bed that his lips had not been wet for the last 24 hours. Others they say were found dead in their beds & from appearances had been dead sometime. They have been dying very fast for the last few weeks but at present the number is decreasing. Only 7 have been reported in the dead house today. This is the lowest number they have had for the last six weeks. We have only lost one and he was in a dying condition when we took charge. All the other poor fellows are doing well. They know not how to express their gratitude to the Sisters for their kind attention to them," Sis. Sophia Gilmeyer wrote.

Sister Mary Garvin

Not everyone was thrilled to see the sisters arrive in Cumberland. They met with some resistance early on because of the anti-Catholic bias in the country at the start of the war, but their devotion to the patients soon won them over.

Sis. Jane Garvin was working in a ward late one night when an ambulance arrived with wounded soldiers. One young soldier had a bad shoulder wound that the surgeon dressed and asked Sis. Jane to watch him through the night. Whenever Sis. Jane approached the soldier, he closed his eyes and pretended to be asleep. The next morning the surgeon redressed the wound with Sis. Jane assisting.

"I assisted all through, but not a word from his lips. He avoided my every look. I plainly perceived he had no love for the Catholic Church or her children," Sis. Jane wrote.

The soldier watched her as she went about her work. He

never said a word to her, though. Finally, after a few days, he said to her, "Sister, I would like to be baptized. I have been a very, very bad man." It was a request that she gladly complied with.

The sisters own spiritual needs were taken care of by Father Collins and Redemptorist Fathers who had a monastery on the opposite side of the Potomac River. In order to assist with morning Mass, the sisters had to get up before daybreak to walk to cross the river in order to reach the monastery.

"We were frequently called upon to give the countersign the sentinel being unable to distinguish who we were in the early dawn, and once when the sentinels crossed bayonets upon our breasts the bravest of us trembled," Sis. Ambrosia wrote.

Despite their success at caring for the men and converting others, the Sisters of Charity also experienced the death of the soldiers they cared for.

"Many I think died of broken hearts. Faces and voices haunt me yet, calling for home and dear ones whom they were destined never to behold on earth," Sis. Agnes Phillips wrote.

Sister Sophia Gilmeyer

Such was the state of medical care in those days that it would be another century before battle wounds took more lives than infection and disease during a war.

The sisters weren't left untouched by the death around them either. Years later, Sis. Ambrosia would recall, "Sad and numerous were the scenes we witnessed in these hospitals, and yet this morning none presents itself more vividly in my mind, than the boy-child I might say, who begged so hard for a gooseberry pie. Over and over he did accost me—'Where is my gooseberry pie?' Such a pie, I presume as his own dear distant mother had often made for him. Oh! how those poor fellows missed their mothers, and murmured their names sleeping and waking."

After three months some of the sisters returned to Cincinnati to care for wounded soldiers who were coming into the city from Richmond, Va., and Nashville, Tenn. Other sisters were sent to New Creek, Va. to care for the wounded there.

When the Cumberland Civil War hospitals were consolidated to a single hospital in Clarysville, Md., the canal warehouses eventually returned to being places were canal boats were constructed.

The Battle of Ball's Bluff

A number of Civil War battles and skirmishes took place near the Potomac River and the Chesapeake and Ohio Canal. The most famous of these was the Battle of Antietam, but almost a year earlier the Union and Confederacy fought next to the Potomac River in the Battle of Ball's Bluff.

The Battle of Ball's Bluff was not a major engagement, but it was a major embarrassment to the federal government.

On October 20, 1861, Union Gen. George McClellan ordered Gen. Charles Stone to conduct "a slight demonstration." McClellan wanted to see how the Confederate forces would react to Union forces in Virginia. Their reaction would allow for some estimation of the strength of the Confederate army in the area.

Stone located his men at Edward's Ferry along the canal and had his artillery shell suspected Confederate positions across the Potomac River in Loudoun County, Va. He also sent about 100 men of the 1st Minnesota Infantry across the river just before dusk to try and scout out enemy positions. The Confederates hadn't returned fire, and the Minnesotans hadn't seen any troops.

The Minnesotans returned, and Stone ordered Col. Charles Devens to send a patrol across the river to scout out any enemy positions. Devens was with the 15th Massachusetts Infantry and stationed on Harrison Island in the middle of the river.

Devens sent Capt. Chase Philbrick and nearly two dozen

men to the Virginia side of the river. They climbed Ball's Bluff and began scouting inland. It was near dark and the inexperienced Capt. Philbrick mistook a line of trees for tents and reported that he had seen an unguarded Confederate camp.

Early the next morning when there was sufficient light, Stone sent Devens with 300 men across the river to attach the enemy camp. The 15th Massachusetts found only trees, no enemy camp. Devens reported his mistake to Stone, who ordered the rest of the 15th Massachusetts—another 350 men—to cross the river. They were to join with Deven's men and move towards Leesburg, Va.

Retreating Union soldiers were forced into the Potomac River where many of them drowned. Photo courtesy of Wikimedia Commons.

Col. Edward Baker, who was also a U.S. Senator, was sent to evaluate the situation and either withdraw the troops or send more to join with the 15th Massachusetts. On his way to the river, Baker met a messenger who told him that the 15th Massachusetts had briefly engaged a company of the 17th Mississippi Infantry. Baker quickly ordered reinforcements for the 15th Massachusetts.

As the reinforcements got slowed down on waiting for boats to cross the Potomac River, Devens and his men continued to engage Confederate troops that were also received reinforcements. However, the Confederate reinforcements weren't slowed down by having to wait for a boat to cross the river.

There were not enough boats to carry retreating soldiers across the Potomac River during the Battle of Ball's Bluff. Photo courtesy of Wikimedia Commons.

Devens and his men were forced to withdraw around 2 p.m. When they did so, they ran into Baker and his men.

With their backs to the river and not enough boats to carry the men to the Maryland side quickly, fighting began in earnest.

It continued until dark with the Union troops fleeing down the steep slope of Ball's Bluff into the river at times to try and swim across it. Others piled into the overcrowded boats, only to have some of them capsize.

Baker was killed around 4:30 p.m. He is the only U.S. Senator to have ever been killed in battle.

Although it was a small engagement, it was an embarrassing loss for the Union, in particular, because it needn't have happened. Faulty intelligence had led to bad decisions.

In all, 223 Union soldiers were killed, 226 wounded, and 553 captured. Some of the bodies floated downriver as far as Mt. Vernon. Future Supreme Court Justice Oliver Wendell Holmes, Jr. was a young lieutenant with the 20th Massachusetts Volunteer Infantry at the battle. He was severely wounded, but he survived.'

Ball's Bluff was the third major Union defeat since the war had started six months earlier. That, coupled with the fact that Baker had been a sitting senator, created political repercussions in Washington, D.C. The politicians accused the military leaders of incompetence and decided to take a greater role in the war. They established a Joint Committee on the Conduct of War on December 9, 1861. It was chaired by Benjamin Wade of Ohio who sought to pursue a more-aggressive war plan than President Lincoln.

The Potomac Home Brigade

Francis Thomas was a former Speaker of the House for the Maryland legislature, a former five-term congressman who represented three different districts in Maryland, and a former governor of Maryland. People had spoken of him as a Democratic Party nominee for the President of the United States. He had also served as president of the C&O Canal Company from 1839 to 1941

Though not from Allegany County (now Garrett County), it was in Allegany County where he had chosen to retreat after his term as governor had ended following his defeat for re-election. A nasty and public divorce led him to live the life of a recluse in the mountains until patriotism stirred his soul.

"Francis Thomas came down from his farm retreat on the Seventeen Mile Grade to rouse the citizenry of Allegany County," J. William Hunt wrote in the *Cumberland Sunday Times* in 1956.

First, Thomas sought and received authorization from the federal government to raise a military unit. In July 1861, Secretary of War Simon Cameron authorized Thomas to raise four regiments "for the protection of the Canal and of the property and persons of loyal citizens of the neighborhood and be stationed in the vicinity of the neighborhood," Thomas Scharf wrote in *History of Western Maryland.*

Thomas had the authorization printed on handbills and published in *The Civilian and Telegraph* newspaper. Then he began a campaign of public speeches in the area to rouse patriotic spirit and encourage men to enlist in the new brigade.

He also met with local officials and civic groups to encourage them to support the formation of the military companies.

Francis Thomas, a former Maryland governor and president of the C&O Canal Company, formed the Potomac Home Brigade in 1861. Photo courtesy of Wikimedia Commons.

During one of Thomas's speeches in August, Confederate sympathizers heckled him. Upset at the disruption, "a large crowd of men at once made a descent on the office of 'The Alleganian,' which was Southern in its sympathies. The office was wholly destroyed, the material being thrown out the window," William Lowdermilk wrote in *History of Cumberland.*

His energy and enthusiasm inspired hundreds of men to enlist as the Second Regiment Potomac Home Brigade, which was organized in the Allegany County from Aug. 21 to Oct. 31, 1861. Of the 10 companies in the brigade, nine were made up of Allegany County men, who signed up to serve three years.

"The military spirit ran high (especially) in Lonaconing and several important meetings were held and one in particular was notable," James Thomas and Judge T.J.C. Williams wrote in *History of Allegany County.* During that meeting, Dr. G. Ellis Porter, caught up in the spirit of the evening, climbed onto a table and gave a speech urging the men in attendance to help defend the Union cause. The men of Lonaconing responded and joined up in large numbers and Porter became a major in the Second Brigade.

The men of the Second Brigade initially fell under the command of Gen. Benjamin Kelley who was charged with protecting the B&O Railroad and its property. Though the brigade didn't begin its official service as a unit until January 1862, as companies formed and were equipped, they were used as needed. Soldiers of the Second Brigade were engaged in skirmishes against Confederate forces as early as August 1861.

During much of their enlistment the soldiers of the Potomac Home Brigade lived according their name and served along the Potomac River from New Creek (Keyser), W.Va.. to east of Cumberland. They patrolled the C&O Canal. They were involved in skirmishes in Springfield, W.Va.; Charlestown, W.Va.; Burlington, W.Va.; Moorfield Junction, W.Va. and Ridgeville, W.Va.

During one of their more-notable excursions, the Second Regiment was part of the army commanded by Gen. David Hunter in 1864 that burned Southern homes in the Shenandoah Valley southward until reaching Lynchburg, Va. The army also pursued the army of Confederate General Jubal Early into the South after the Battle of the Monocacy in 1864.

By the time the Civil War ended, 94 soldiers in the Second Brigade had been killed. This represented about 9 percent of the brigade's complement of men. Of those 94 men, one officer had been killed in action, nine enlisted men had been killed and action and the remainder died from disease or wounds, according to *History and Roster of the Maryland Volunteers.*

"That the Second (Regiment) Potomac Home Brigade fully sustained the reputation of Maryland soldiers for bravery and fidelity will never be questioned," Scharf wrote.

Allegany County also contributed significantly to the formation of the Third Regiment Potomac Home Brigade. This regiment started forming right after the Second Regiment filled up on Oct. 31, 1861, and continued recruiting until May 20, 1862. Of the 10 companies in this regiment, four were formed with men of Allegany County.

Stanton's Navy

When Chesapeake and Ohio Canal boatmen traveled to Georgetown at the start of the 1862 boating season, they were surprised to find the federal government confiscating their boats. They had come to suspect such actions from Confederate raiders over the previous year but not from the people who were supposed to be protecting the canal.

The battle between the ironclads, the *U.S.S. Monitor* and the *C.S.S. Virginia* (formerly the *U.S.S. Merrimac)*, at Hampton Roads, Va., on March 8 had left the Union government officials shaken and scared. News quickly reached Washington, D.C., that the *Virginia* had sunk both the *U.S.S. Cumberland* and *U.S.S. Congress* with relative ease.

What was to stop the *Virginia* from sailing up the Potomac River and bombarding Washington?

Secretary of War Edwin Stanton feared that a single Confederate ironclad could destroy the Union Navy and take Fort Monroe at Hampton Roads.

"Likely the first movement of the Merrimac would be to come up the Potomac and disperse Congress, destroy the Capitol and public buildings; or she might go to New York or Boston and destroy those cities, or levy from them sufficient to carry on the war," Secretary of the Navy Gideon Welles wrote in his diary.

President Abraham Lincoln was so worried that "he could not deliberate or be satisfied with the opinions of non-professional men, but ordered his carriage and drove to the navy yard to see and consult with Admiral [John] Dahlgren [the officer in charge of the Washington Navy Yard] and other naval officers, who might be there," Welles wrote.

The Battle of the Ironclads at Hampton Roads scared federal officials into confiscating canal boats. Photo courtesy of the Library of Congress.

On March 9, Quartermaster General Montgomery C. Meigs and Admiral Dahlgren, not knowing the *Monitor* had fought the *Virginia* to a standstill, issued orders to seize fifty or sixty canal boats. The plan was to fill them with stone and gravel and sink them at Kettle Bottom Shoals or other points on the Potomac River to prevent the *Virginia* from reaching Washington.

Canallers had already fought off a Union Army plan to take their boats. In February, Major General Nathaniel P. Banks' advance guard crossed the Potomac River and occupied Harpers Ferry, Va. The troops needed to be supplied, but the Baltimore and Ohio Railroad bridge needed repairs because Confederate troops had torn up the tracks to prevent trains from coming into the south.

The *U.S.S. Monitor* fought *C.S.S. Virginia* to a standstill in 1862, which helped save dozens of canal boats from being sunk. Photo courtesy of the Library of Congress.

A pontoon bridge made of canal boats was proposed at Sandy Hook. Supplies could be brought to the Union troops across the bridge, allowing time for the B&O Railroad bridge to be rebuilt.

Boats had been confiscated for the project, but when Gen. George McClellan had visited the area on Feb. 27, he decided the banks were too steep for the project and the plans were scrapped.

And now, the canallers were having to deal with another Union attempt to take their boats. These boats were business investments that had cost them around $1,500. The boats were the canallers' means to make a living. Even if they were reimbursed the cost of the boat, how would they live while they waited for another boat to be built?

Workers began loading the confiscated boats with gravel and by nightfall on Mar. 9, eight of the boats were ready to sail to the Kettle Bottom Shoals. The boats set sail the next morning, but that evening word reached Washington that the battle of the ironclads at Hampton Roads had been a draw.

The news appeased government officials somewhat. "On the basis of this report, Welles succeeded in getting Lincoln to forbid the sinking of any of the 60 canal boats that had been loaded with gravel and sent down to Kettle Bottom Shoals as long as the Monitor could keep the Merrimac from entering the Potomac," Canal Historian Harlan Unrau wrote in his *Historic Resource Study: Chesapeake and Ohio Canal.*

Even after this crisis subsided, the military continued to rush canal boats to Washington. On Mar. 10, some 103 canal barges, most of which were empty, passed through Williamsport, Md., under the charge of army officers. Of this fleet of boats, thirty-seven had come from Cumberland, Md., and the rest from unknown points, according to a letter in the C&O Canal Company records dated Mar. 10.

Weeks later, Lincoln, Stanton, and other officials rode a steamer down the Potomac River to Fort Monroe and saw a long line of canal boats moored along the shore. According to Welles, Lincoln jokingly said, "That is Stanton's navy. That is the fleet concerning which he and Mr. Welles became so excited in my room. Welles was incensed and opposed the scheme, and it has proved that Neptune was right. Stanton's navy is as useless as the paps of a man to a suckling child. They may be some show to amuse the child, but they are good for nothing for service."

In all, the government held 103 canal boats for more than a month. This represented nearly two-thirds of the boats on the canal, and it nearly crippled commerce on the canal.

In late April, officials found a use for half of the boats.

They were taken downriver to be used as pontoon bridges for Union troops to cross the Rappahannock River into Fredericksburg, Va.

The pontoon bridge made of canal boats across the Rappahannock River used by the Union Army to enter Fredericksburg. Photo courtesy of the National Park Service.

A.C. Greene, one of the canal company directors, wrote to the C&O Canal Company complaining that between the military actions against the canal and bad weather, "There has be no real navigation on the canal this year." He added that the "very existence of the canal" was "trembling in the balance." It would be impossible for the boatmen to replace in 1862 the boats held by the government.

The other half of the boats not used at the Rappahannock River were eventually returned to their owners to resume trade on the canal.

C&O Canal President Imprisoned for Treason

Rule of thumb: Never say anything out loud or in writing that you don't want other people to know. It was a rule that Alfred Spates, president of the C&O Canal during the Civil War, apparently never learned even after he was arrested three times during the war.

When the Civil War started, President Abraham Lincoln was heavy handed with Maryland in order to keep the state in the Union. If he hadn't been, there's a good chance that Washington D. C. might have found itself in the Confederate States. As part of this heavy-handedness, high-level Confederate sympathizers in Maryland were arrested and imprisoned. Among these was Thomas McKaig, a state senator from Cumberland, Md.

The first time that Spates ran afoul of the federal government is believed to have been after the September 1862 Battle of Antietam, according to Harlan Unrau in *The Chesapeake and Ohio Canal During the Civil War: 1861-1865.* Spates wasn't arrested but he was detained for questioning.

On July 6, 1863, Spates was trapped in Hagerstown, Md., when the Confederate Army retreating from Gettysburg, Pa., took control of the city from the Union Cavalry. Spates met with Confederate Lt. Gen. Richard Ewell "regarding the damages to the canal, and that he had obtained a pass to cross Confederate lines directly from General Lee," Timothy Snyder wrote in *Trembling in the Balance.*

Later in the month, Spates was in Baltimore and told a group of men he knew that he had visited Gen. Robert E. Lee in Hagerstown. One of the men in the group, William H. Hoffman, reported the story to the Provost Marshal. Hoffman was a former congressman and treasurer of the C&O Canal Company. Spates believed that Hoffman said something because he wanted to become president of the C&O Canal.

The Provost Marshal questioned Spates and released him. Spates wrote a lctter to the Provost Marshal in late August proclaiming his innocence, but he was still rearrested on Sept. 1. Spates posted bond and was released in mid-September.

Spates trial before a military tribunal began on September 16, 1863, and lasted three weeks. During that time, he was imprisoned in Fort McHenry. The tribunal found him guilty of crossing Confederate lines and communicating with the enemy on December 4, 1863, but Spates was found not guilty of giving aid and intelligence to the enemy. The guilty charge was enough to see him sentenced to spend the rest of the war in the prison at Fort Warren in Boston Harbor.

Spates made an appeal to Assistant Secretary of War Peter Watson in the hopes of getting Secretary of War Edwin Stanton to pardon him. Spates wrote, "I went to Washington County to put the Chesapeake and Ohio Canal in order—and did—for the use of the Government and Genl. Kelly [sic] now here will state I did and he used it."

The appeal worked and Spates' sentence was overturned in January 1864.

Following his release, Spates returned to his position as president of the C&O Canal Company.

During this time, Spates also served as president of the Cumberland City Bank. Following the war, he served as a Maryland state senator from Allegany County.

THE CANAL IN OPERATION

More Than One Way to Move Coal

At the turn of the 19th century, canals were quite popular in the United States. The country was expanding westward and those people wanted a way to bring their products to where the bulk of the population was in the east. Canal popularity peaked in 1850, which is also the same year the C&O Canal reached Cumberland. There were 4,000 miles of canal in the U.S. with the C&O making up nearly 5 percent of that amount.

The reason people other than George Washington were interested in building canals was that Americans were pushing west from the coastline. In 1800, 19 percent of the U.S. population lived west of the Alleghenies. By 1830, it was up to 27 percent of the population. These people needed goods from the east that they couldn't find on the frontier and they needed to be able to ship their goods to the eastern cities and seaports.

The question was how to get move those items between the two points.

The construction on the National Road from Cumberland, Md., to Vandalia, Ill., started in 1811. It was a slow route, plagued by maintenance problems. Even so, it was faster than the mash-up of roads and turnpikes one would have to take otherwise. It was its era's interstate.

The National Road was completed to Wheeling, Va., in 1818. It was 30 times more expensive to move goods along the road than by a canal. It was estimated at the time that four horses could pull one-ton by wagon for twelve miles in one day. However, on a canal, those same four horses could pull 100 tons twenty-four miles in a day.

The Chesapeake and Ohio Canal was America's "Great National Project" of the early 19th century.

The Cushwa Coal and Brick Warehouse in Williamsport. Photo courtesy of the National Park Service.

Coal is considered the lifeblood of the canal, but that is not the only cargo that was carried on the C&O Canal, particularly in its early years. One toll rate chart for the canal lists rates for fifty-five different types of cargo. The chart includes the expected cargo of coal, as well as similar items like coke and charcoal. However, you'll also find crops such as corn, flax, and potatoes. Boats also carried livestock, bacon, and fish.

Confederate raiders went after canal boats during the Civil War. Most of the time they were hoping to find the holds full of something edible. If they were thirsty, some boats also carried whiskey. One could even find cargoes of horses and carriages.

The nice thing about transporting other items on the canal is that it would usually be stored in a way that made it easier to load and offload, such as barrels. Coal, on the other hand, had to be shoveled out of the holds and stirred up a lot of coal dust to make everything in the family cabin dark with soot.

Canal boat captains were charged by the ton and mile. For example, a load of 110 tons of coal in 1841 would have cost the captain $202.40 to transport (110 tons x .01 ton-mile x 184 miles). The captain would be given a way bill from the wharfmaster at the start of his journey, and he would pay it at the way house at Georgetown.

Since the canal opened each time a new dam was built to impound water for it, prices tended to drop as more of the canal opened for navigation. Still using coal as an example, the cost dropped from 1 cent per ton-mile in 1834 to ¼ cent per ton-mile in 1851.

Fierce competition with the railroad also caused downward pressure on prices. This was great for the captain who had to pay the tolls, but hard on both the railroad and canal.

"During their rivalry for the flour trade, the railroad had raised its rates and its directors urged the canal company to do likewise," Elizabeth Kytle wrote in *Home on the Canal*.

The canal company must have seen this collusion as a way to earn back some of its lost profits and followed suit.

"When the canal company responded to this gambit by doing so [lowering their tolls], the railroad put its rates even lower than before and within a few months the canal company's flour trade was in sorry condition," Kytle wrote.

Coal slowly took over the business of the canal. Part of the reason was in competition with the railroad, the canal was the most-efficient carrier. Another reason is that the Western Maryland coal companies started operating their own boats to carry their coal to Washington, D.C.

Western Maryland coal mines provided the major cargo for the C&O Canal. Photo courtesy of the Albert and Angela Feldstein Collection.

Of the 101,950 tons of cargo hauled on the canal in 1850, 7,956 tons or 7.8 percent was coal. Nearly four times as much flour was carried along the canal that year. However, by 1875 (the canal's peak year, as far as tonnage hauled) 904,898 tons of the 973,805 total tons hauled was coal. This is 92.9 percent of the canal's business that year.

One other interesting note concerns how the captain's paid for their tolls. Nowadays, it seems unthinkable to believe that the way bills could have been paid with anything other than U.S. currency.

This was not the case when the Patowmack Company operated. While early tolls listed were in British pounds, it wasn't the only currency used in the early United States. The Patomack Company had to create a conversion chart for tolls were paid in: Spanish pieces of eight, silver coins, French crowns, Johannes, Moidores, English guineas, French guineas, English crowns, doubloons, Spanish pistols, French pistols, Arabian chequins, or gold coins. All of which were in circulation in the early 19th century.

Are Two Boats Better Than One?

When the Chesapeake and Ohio Canal first fully opened in 1850, the canal boats were pulled by hardworking mules. When the canal finally closed in 1924, the boats were still pulled by mules. The canal failed to evolve during a period of innovation in America.

It wasn't that the canal couldn't evolve. Other canals did. It was that the C&O Canal couldn't do it efficiently.

The C&O Canal Company had been interested in using steam engines instead of canal mules even before the canal opened to Cumberland, Md. Canal President Charles Mercer talked about the use of steamboats on the canal during the company's first annual meeting in 1829.

The company's first chief engineer had considered it as well, at least for small packet boats. He also pointed out the major problem with doing so. The engine would take up space on the boat, and it would generate a lot of heat.

As European canals began to adapt steam engines for use on their waterways, the C&O Canal Company continued showing cautious interest. The first rules and regulations for the canal didn't allow for steam-powered boats on the canal, but in 1833, the company decided that it would suspend tolls for a year for the company that developed a steam packet boat that could travel at a "speed of which shall not be less than eight miles per hour," Harlan Unrau wrote in *Historic Resource Study: Chesapeake and Ohio Canal.*

Nothing came of this challenge, and steam continued to be absent from the canal even as it began appearing on other

American canals, such as the Chesapeake and Delaware Canal and the Delaware and Raritan Canal.

Even as steam engines evolved to eliminate some of the earlier problems that the canal engineer had worried about, steamboat didn't appear on the canal until the 1840s, according to Unrau. It was used to for Samuel W. Dewey's packet service and Lemuel Williams freight boats. They did not last long.

According to the *Cumberland Daily Times*, the first successful steamer was the "Cathcart," built by J. L. Cathcart, of Georgetown, and launched in 1857.

"The 'Cathcart' was run by two small engines with one propeller," the newspaper reported. "The shaft was constructed with a universal joint, and ran through the rudder post, so that by a simple plan of manipulation the propeller was made to steer the boat. The carrying capacity of the 'Cathcart' was about 100 tons, and as a specimen of her speed, it is recorded that she made three round trips inside of 22 days.The boat operated on the canal for four or five years until it was burned by Rebel soldiers near Alexandria, Va.

If it hadn't been burned, it probably would have been banned. By the start of the Civil War, the canal company wanted to ban steamboats because it was believed that the wake they caused damaged the canal berm.

"Generally speaking, however, the issue of whether steamboats with their greater speed definitively did or did not damage berms was never ultimately laid to rest," Karen Gray wrote in her article, "Steamboats on the C&O Canal."

The company initially tried to ban steam engine use on the canal, but a petition convinced the directors otherwise. However, they imposed special rules for steamboats on the canal. Boats could not travel more than four miles per hour and could draw no more than three feet of water. Freight boats would also have the right of way over packet boats. Packet boats would have to start paying tolls, which created a financial burden for them.

Packet service on the canal waned by 1870 as people opted to travel by rail, which wasn't hindered by a speed limit.

About the time that steam-packet boats disappeared from the canal, steam-powered freight service began. Separate experiments with it had taken place in the 1850s and 1860s, but it didn't take hold until the 1870s.

"Beginning in 1873 with one boat, the steam fleet had grown to 16 by 1878," Gray wrote. "Of those 16, a dozen were owned by coal companies and the remaining four were apparently privately owned. In 1879, there were 19 steam freighters that made 272 trips on the canal, carrying a total of 26,428 tons of coal."

The steamers tended to make a lot of news because of their faster speed.

In 1879, Canal Superintendent E. Mulvaney conducted his own experiments with steam freight and double boats on the canal. The goal was to find cheaper ways to carry freight on the canal and make it more attractive to shippers.

He had difficulty at first steering two boats "fitted with the double steering apparatus of the pulley power," he wrote in a letter to Canal President A. P. Gorman. Once Mulvaney got the hang of it, things went fine and he made nine trips.

He discovered the labor costs running two boats together were cut in half because only one crew was needed for the two boats. "But they have to be taken apart at the locks and passed through single which necessitates the carrying of a double crew and team for use at these points. The benefits or economy of this system of boating over that of running them apart cannot with the present condition of the locks be taken advantage of," Mulvaney wrote.

Double boats traveled on many canals and were tested on the C&O Canal. They would have appeared much like these double boats on the Erie Canal.

While Mulvaney seemed to think this a big hindrance, a *Cumberland Daily Times* article made the locking through of double boats seem simple. "A short distance above the locks the New Era glided over to the Maryland bank and there parted with her partner, which was at once taken charge of by two fiery mules and swung through the locks in a jiffy," the newspaper reported. "In a short time the New Era followed and went through the lock in five minutes, though that time is by no means a fair sample of her average time in locking, for athwart the mouth of the lock was an obstruction which was difficult to get by. There was no cramping or jamming in the lock, the engines letting her out at once."

The speed that a steamer-towed canal coat could travel was often compared to the speed the boat pulled by five or six mules. It could typically make the entire trip down the canal in just over four days.

That's not to say that there weren't problems. In Cumberland, a steamer was going to be used to tow a canal boat loaded with coal. "The steamer was attached by a large chain to a neighboring boat, but so great was the power of propulsion that the steamer snapped the chain and shot away some distance down the canal before she could be stopped," the *Daily Times* reported.

The biggest problem most canallers saw with using steam engines on boats was that they consumed an average of eight tons of coal on a trip. This cut into the canallers' profits for each trip. Some boats were said to have nearly cut that amount in half and this came from reducing the weight of the equipment. However, that meant the boat owner was paying for 4.5 tons of coal that he wouldn't be paid for at the end of the trip.

In his experiments with steam freight, Mulvaney had a steamboat tow one and two boats. He also had a single and double boat pulled by a team of four mules. His conclusion was that to make the best use of steam or double boats "some improvement of the canal is necessary in order to increase the tonnage so that coal can be freighted at the present rates."

For double boating to work, Mulvaney estimated that all of the locks should be lengthened so that time would not be lost by coupling and uncoupling boats in order for them to pass through the locks. He also recommended raising the banks of the canal so that the depth of water could be increased a foot, which in turn would allow boats to increase their draft and take on heavier loads of coal.

The most effective combination to yield the greatest profit was to have a steamboat tow two boats with a two mule reserve team to help at the locks. Using this method, 3.5 trips could be made compared to three trips made by a single boat pulled by four mules. The big difference is that the double steam boat method carried 215 tons of coal each trip. The final estimate was that the double boat steam method had net earnings of $97.09 compared to a double boat pulled by four mules, which had net earnings of $87.48. A steamboat pulling a single boat had earnings of $54.97 and a single boat pulled by four mules had earnings of $38.36.

Despite the increased earnings, it was not a transportation method that continued being used on the canal.

It should also be noted that there were failed experiments with navigation innovations on the canal.

One inventor built a ship that was propelled by something that resembled a duck's foot.

Another person tried to create an air-powered canal boat. Two large windmill fans were installed on the Peter Quigley in 1872. "The model of the boat moved very rapidly through the water, and worked so successfully to all appearances that a man like Mr. A. T. Greene was among those who thought the idea a master-stroke," the *Daily Times* reported. "When it came to practical application, though the fans revolved at a wonderful rate of speed, the boat would not move more than about a mile or so an hour."

The Georgetown Incline Plane

Following the Civil War, the canal entered its golden years beginning around 1870. During this time, an estimated 500 boats worked on the canal. "The very idea of this number of boat in a waterway the size of the canal they lived and worked on taxes the powers of belief of some surviving boatmen," Elizabeth Kytle wrote in *Home on the Canal.*

The canal started to look like Route 15 during rush hour, instead of exits there were backups at locks and lots of traffic moving slowly. Canal President James C. Clark reported that "often a string of loaded boats from half mile to a mile in length is seen lying above the Collector's Office in Georgetown, waiting their turn to get in to the wharves to discharge their cargoes." This meant sixty to eighty boats could be backed up at Georgetown. Captains were finding they had to tie up further and further from Georgetown, encountering longer and longer delays. Just as with traffic today, this meant a lot of lost time. And lost time meant lost income for canallers.

Actually, a backup on the canal might not quite look that way along the route. This is because the boats needed to be spread out so that when a boat slowed to go into a lock it wasn't rammed from behind by another boat. Since it took a while for a loaded boat to slow down or turn, a captain needed time to avoid other boats, which meant that space was needed.

All of that income from tolls rolled into the canal

company and the company even made progress against its outstanding loans and interest.

During the 1870s, canal boats could back up for a mile along the C&O Canal. Photo courtesy of the National Park Service.

Although Georgetown was where the canal ended, it wasn't the final destination for every canal boat. Some simply needed to get into the Potomac River and the only way to do that was through the tidelock in the city.

Realizing this, the canal company began searching for ways to bypass Georgetown. The idea of building river locks above the Alexandria Aqueduct was first discussed during the Civil War.

The idea was simple, but its execution wasn't. Where the boats backed up along the canal was thirty-nine feet above the river.

The canal company was under court order to pay down its debt and could not afford to take on the new project.

The Potomac Lock and Dock Company eventually took up the challenge in 1872. It was soon decided that using typical lift locks to get boats from the canal to the river would require too much water.

William Hutton, chief engineer for the canal company came up with the idea of using an incline plane. He then consulted with Potomac Lock and Dock on the best way to build it.

What they came up with was essentially a lock on wheels. The *Cumberland Alleganian* described the incline plane this way:

> "The opening through which the boats are floated into the caisson is in the bank of the canal, closed on the inside next to the canal by a lift gate; and closed on the inside next to the river by a drop gate, when closed fitting closely into shoulders of masonry on either side of the opening, and when opened to allow the egress of boats lays upon the bottom of the lock. An incline plane 600 feet long runs from this outer gate into the bed of the river below; this plane carries three tracks. Upon the center track, the caisson which carries the boats down travels; the two side tracks are used for heavily loaded counterpoises, which sustain and balance the weight of the caisson and its load; the caisson is a hollow vessel of iron plate, large enough to contain a boat. This caisson is placed upon three large trucks, which are graduated so as to keep the caisson level, (the rear truck being the highest.) It is connected with a counterpoise on either side by huge iron chains which pass from the counterpoises over iron pulleys and are attached to the forward end of the caisson. It is provided with a water tight iron gate, which is raised up to allow the ingress and egress of the

boats; a ratchet arrangement is attached to the lower side, which is intended to catch and stay the caisson in its descent in case the carrying chains break. The pulley wheels are moved by hydraulic pressure which is furnished by a large turbine wheel placed under the forward or upper end of the plane. The caisson fits closely into a wooden frame lined with gum packing, which is set into a sill of masonry forming the outer edge of the lock.

"When a boat is to be lowered into the river, the caisson is raised to the level of the lock and its forward end fitted into the frame described above. The inner gate of the lock is then raised, the outer gate lowered back into the lock, and the boat glides into the caisson; the lock gates are then closed, and the gate of the caisson lowered to its place; the caisson then glides slowly and evenly down the incline until it is submerged in the waters of the river below, when the boat floats off, and the caisson ascends for another load."

The caisson was 112 feet long and nearly seventeen feet wide.

The entire process was said to be done in six minutes, comparable to locking through a regular lift lock. Other reports say that it took twelve to eighteen minutes.

When the Georgetown Incline Plane was completed it was largest structure of its kind and it was considered an engineering marvel. A scale model was displayed at the 1878 Paris Exposition. Nearly as soon as it went into operation, however it became non-essential.

The Georgetown Incline Plane caisson (at the top of the photo) could carry boats down a hill from the canal to the Potomac River. Photo courtesy of the National Park Service.

"As fate would have it, tonnage on the canal was dropping by this time and the congestion that had created the need for the incline was rarely a problem. Still, the incline operated more or less constantly until late 1879 when it began to be used only on those occasions when the Rock Creek outlet was inadequate or dysfunctional," Karen Gray wrote in the article "The Georgetown Canal Incline: Its Ups & Downs."

The sheer size of the incline plane brought out critics who were proven right in one instance.

In 1876, the caisson slammed against the headwall when the counterweights were adjusted. This caused some slight cracking, but it wasn't thought important enough to report. The following spring the caisson was descending with a fully loaded boat when one of the masonry anchors for a winding pulley pulled free. The wire ropes were released, shearing off axles. The counterweights slid down their tracks and smashed into the lower wall.

"Amazingly, the caisson and the boat it carried were not damaged, but three men were killed: Assistant harbormaster John Mead who was crushed by a counterweight, and two other incline workers who were struck by the lashing cables," Gray wrote.

Hutton, whose engineering marvel had been praised, was now the target of blame. He made some improvements to the system, including draining the water from the caisson one the boat was inside. This lightened the weight being lowered along the incline plane, but it also meant that the caisson's weight could not be adjusted against the counterweights. That had been done by changing the water level in the caisson.

When an 1880 flood damaged the Rock Creek outlet lock, all boats on the canal were required to use the incline plane. This situation lasted until the 1889 flood destroyed the incline plane.

Little remains today of the incline plane, but there is a wayside exhibit at mile 2.26 where the incline plane was located to explain how it worked.

Coxey's Army Marches on Washington

On April 14, 1894, the invasion the residents of Frostburg, Md., had been expecting for weeks happened. Coxey's Army appeared at the crest of Federal Hill and marched into town right down Main Street.

"At 4:15 p.m., the marshal of the marching group, a four piece band, flags and banners, and some wagons, followed by a group of 245 tired and bedraggled mortals, crossed Federal Hill and marched in a more or less soldierly fashion down Main Street into Frostburg," Harold Scott wrote in his book *Incredible, Strange, Unusual...*

Coxey's Army was a group of unemployed workers that had formed in Massillon, Ohio, under the direction of Jacob Coxey. The official name of the group was the Commonweal of Christ, but most people referred to it as Coxey's Army. The group planned to march to Washington D.C. where Coxey would present his petition to Congress of his ideas for a national program of building and repairing roads that would also solve the national unemployment problem. The group had started its march with much fanfare, leaving Massillon on Easter Sunday, Mar. 25, and had since then made their way slowly eastward.

"Stories of pillaging, disorderly conduct, and even assaults by the band of men all served to alarm the local residents and spread fear and apprehension as to what the impending invasion would bring. Some news accounts were reporting that the army was infested with drunks, crooks, and toughs," Scott wrote.

Jacob Coxey, founder of the Commonweal of Christ. Photo courtesy of Wikimedia Commons.

While the actual situation was not that bad, the army did face deprivation and slow passage on the very roads they hoped to repair.

Infighting over leadership of the group had led to factions forming within it and even a mutiny as the two leaders vied for control of the army. Carl Browne, who had been appointed by Coxey to lead the group, was ousted from leadership and a group led by Unknown Smith took control. No one knew the man's name and he refused to give it to reporters so they called him "Unknown Smith."

Dismissed from the group, Browne reached Frostburg first. Though the group was named after Coxey, he rarely traveled with it. Instead he traveled ahead and slept in rooms while the men who followed him were generally forced to sleep outside. Browne's first move on reaching Frostburg was to telegraph Coxey about the incident. Reporters waiting for the army to arrive learned of what had happened and word spread of the mutiny.

Coxey's Army on the move in their march toward Washington, D.C. Photo courtesy of Wikimedia Commons.

So it was when the army marched through town, the city officials were expecting trouble, according to John Grant in his monograph, *Coxey's 38-Day March Through the Alleghenies in Search of Economic Justice.*

A week before the army's arrival, the Frostburg City Council voted to spend $100 to help accommodate the group. On the day of the army's arrival, citizens took up a collection to feed them and arrangements were made to allow them to sleep in Ravenscroft's Opera House. The city also hired special police officers to help maintain order should the rumors of rowdiness prove to be true.

The expected violence didn't happen when the army arrived. The marchers were tired and hungry. Some suffered from exposure.

The group dubbed the Frostburg stop as Camp Robert E. Lee and started campfires in a vacant lot near the opera house and cooked their evening meals. When the evening shows were over in the opera house, the men went to their accommodations on the third floor.

The following day Coxey arrived from Cumberland, Md., to settle the authority dispute between Browne and Smith.

He first praised the group for their efforts to date and added, "The eyes of sixty-five million people are fixed on this noble and patriotic band, and on the success of our movement depends the future happiness of a great people," according to the *Cumberland Evening Times.*

He then called for got a vote to expel from Smith from the group. Browne was restored and the march was ready to continue. Despite their troubles and trials on the march, most of the men still shared Coxey's vision to change government policy.

Coxey's Army left Frostburg at 9 a.m. and headed for Cumberland where it became Coxey's Navy.

The group arrived at Camp Victory in Lavale, Md., around noon. Camp Victory was a Narrows Park baseball field just outside of Cumberland. According to the *Cumberland Evening Times*, the day's weather was beautiful and brought out hundreds of spectators to watch the army arrive.

"The ball field had a fence around it, which created a chance to collect an admission fee to see the army in camp. This had been done successfully at the Exposition Park near Pittsburgh. On Sunday, April 15, 1500 citizens of Cumberland paid 10 cents to see the army prepare its camp in the ball park," Grant wrote.

Cumberland residents contributed food to the army that included six barrels of corn, ten bales of hay, three quarters of beef, 600 loaves of bread, 140 pounds of bologna, seventy-five pounds of cheese and sixty pounds of coffee.

Scott wrote, "...some of the news accounts from Cumberland, noted that although there were some earnest, good men within the army who were out of work and seeking some intervention or program by the Federal Government that would insure jobs in the future, if those spectators who visited the park in the Narrows in Cumberland expected to find a large body of men, with a glorious mission, men determined to stand by their principals at all cost, they no doubt were disappointed. For the most part all they found was a sorry looking bunch of weary, footsore humans, who had very little idea of what their glorious mission and objectives were in marching."

The men rested for the rest of the day at the camp and all through the next day. The time was used to repair equipment, mend clothing, and get haircuts. Scott wrote that during a morning baseball game, "The Working Men" defeated "The Hobos."

Behind this much-needed rest, the leaders of the group,

Coxey and Browne, were facing a tough choice. The group has started its march with much fanfare, leaving Massillon on Easter Sunday, Mar. 25, and had since then made their way slowly eastward. The journey had thus far been tough on the men and they were averaging between ten and fifteen miles a day. To the east still lay many mountains to cross and just under two weeks to do it in.

Coxey's Army leaves Cumberland on the *Good Roads* and *J.S. Coxey* on their way to Washington. Photo courtesy of the Library of Congress.

May 1 was the designated date to be in Washington, D.C., where Coxey would present his petition to Congress of his ideas for a national program of building and repairing roads that would also solve the national unemployment problem.

Coxey decided to give his group a boost and he hired two C&O Canal boats to take the army to Williamsport, Md. Tuesday morning, Apr. 17, the group marched through Cumberland to the canal terminus and boarded the boats. "In the crowd was the Consolidated Coal Company freight agent; he had the unique job of deciding what should be the rental fare for the barges. After much calculation and many references to various rate books, he came up with a charge of $89 for Coxey's Army," wrote Grant.

The first boat was renamed "Good Roads" and was commanded by Coxey. It got underway around 12:30 p.m. "Sandy" Leitch supplied travel music on the bagpipes. The second boat, renamed "J.S. Coxey" got started about twenty minutes later. It was commanded by Carl Browne, the man the men had voted to lead them in Frostburg. On this boat, the Commonweal band played the travel music.

The reporters who were covering the event were forced to rent their own boat and follow the army down the canal to Williamsport.

From there, the group was able to meet their deadline date to get to Washington on foot where thousands of people lined the streets to watch them march through the city. However, things still did not go smoothly.

"Before the marchers could present their petition, the police rushed them, and Coxey and the other leaders were arrested for trampling on the grass," Scott wrote.

Though the group failed that day, what they sought to achieve resonated with the public. Fifty years later, Coxey was finally able to read his speech from the Capitol steps. Grant also notes that many of Coxey's ideas became part of President Franklin Delano Roosevelt's New Deal Programs.

Labor Trouble on the C&O Canal

Capt. John Zimmerman had his crew move the canal boat, *Joseph Murray*, under a chute to take on a load of coal from the Maryland Coal Company at the Cumberland, Md., canal basin on August 4, 1873.

He worked with his son and two hands to position the canal boat's open hold under the church. It was something that occurred many times daily at the basin as canal boats prepared to haul coal to Georgetown in the District of Columbia, and 1873 was the height of the canal's "golden age." By the end of the year, ninety-one canal boats would be built in Cumberland, bringing the number of boats navigating the canal up to 500, each with an average capacity of 112 tons.

The problem was that the Maryland Coal Company hadn't agreed to pay the uniform rate of freight that the canallers were insisting upon to offset increase hauling costs including a five cents per ton toll increase that had been raised in February. Though the canallers were unionized, they had agreed to not haul freight on their boats for companies that wouldn't pay the uniform rate.

Zimmerman knew that he was breaking with his fellow canallers, but he had "boasted that he would let no man stop him," according to the *Cumberland Daily Times*.

He had not tried to hide when he left the Maryland Coal Company office and headed for the *Joseph Murray*. Nor had he been secretive when he moved the boat under the coal chutes.

The other canallers knew what he was doing and they didn't like it.

"Hardly had the first pot of coal touched the bottom of the hold before the deck of the 'Joseph Murray' swarmed with boarders. Zimmerman made a show of resistance but was shoved off into the canal; his son and the other members of the crew leaving the vessel without further notice," the *Cumberland Daily Times* reported.

Boats in the Cumberland canal basin waiting to head to Georgetown with their holds filled with coal. Photo courtesy of the National Park Service.

The mob then chopped the stern post and destroyed windows on cabins. As they prepared to move onto other areas of the boat, someone realized that the canal boat belonged to Dave Eckelberry of Hancock and not Zimmerman. He was only employed by Eckelberry to captain the boat.

They stopped their destruction, but not their taunting of Zimmerman.

"While Zimmerman was struggling in the water, he was pelted with lumps of coal," the newspaper reported.

He got out of the water and walked dripping wet to the office of the Maryland Coal Company. He took out his wallet and removed the money to dry and return it to the company agent in the office. Zimmerman had been paid extra to haul the coal for the company.

The other canallers swarmed into the office and swore at and threatened Alexander Ray, the company agent from Georgetown. "No blows were struck, however, and the demonstration ended in noise," the newspaper reported.

Zimmerman left the office and headed into Cumberland. The crowd of canallers followed him and jeered him.

For Zimmerman, enough was enough. He "turned about, drew a revolver and threatened to shoot," according to the newspaper.

Someone was able to knock the pistol from his hand while Joseph Kirtley ran off to issue a complaint against Zimmerman. A warrant was issued for Zimmerman's arrest. He was taken before the magistrate, but eventually released on bail.

Captain Mills and other Cumberland police officers were sent to wharf to "quell any disturbance that might be in progress or that might arise, but on their arrival everything was quiet, and remained so throughout the day, although no other boat attempted to load for the Maryland Coal Company," the *Cumberland Daily News* reported.

The Maryland Coal Company eventually shipped 110,663 tons of coal in 1873 or 14 percent of Cumberland's business that year. It shipped the third-largest amount (out of 11 companies) in 1873.

THE LAST YEARS

The Spong Family Tragedy

Samuel Spong had boated through the night and brought Canal Boat No. 74 into Georgetown early in the morning of September 11, 1916. Once he had locked through to the river, Samuel and his oldest son, Thomas, brought the mules aboard, and a tug boat towed them to a spot where they could tie up until later in the morning when they could offload their coal.

They tied up to the sea wall of the Capital Traction power house around 5:30 a.m. They were near a six-inch steam exhaust pipe that came from the power house underground, exited through the sea wall, and then turned down into the river.

Samuel and Thomas went into the mule shed at the front of the boat to brush the mules and feed them. Then they would remove the hatch covers so that the coal could be removed from the holds. Meanwhile, Nina Spong woke up and started to prepare for breakfast. The other Spong children, John, 13; Willard, 11; and Sarah, 6; were still asleep.

At 6 a.m., Edgar Rollins, a fireman at the power house, turned the steam from one of the three boilers into the pipe to blow off steam. It was something that he did every morning before the fires were started in the power house and the boilers reached full heat.

"The high pressure of the steam in the pipe caused a flange on the pipe, where it turned downward into the water, to blow off. The escaping steam went directly into the cabin of the boat," the *Washington Star* reported.

There was no time for the Spongs in the family cabin to

escape. They awoke to scalding steam.

"The cries of the mother and children attracted the father, who was on another part of the boat," the newspaper reported.

He and Thomas ran back to the other end of the boat to help.

Boats waiting to unload their cargoes near Georgetown. Photo courtesy of the National Park Service.

Nina, who was already awake, was able to run out of the cabin, but the children weren't so lucky. They screamed as they were scalded.

"Then came steam, steam, steam, literally cooking my family to death," Samuel said at the cornoner's inquest.

He attempted to run into the cabin, but had his back

scalded. Thomas pulled him out of the cabin and entered himself, although he did so carefully. As he located one of his brothers or sister, he would carry his siblings back to the door and pass them out to Samuel.

"There was one little fellow we just couldn't get out. He came running to the window with his face in agony, crying bitterly," Samuel said.

An employee on the shore heard the family screaming, and called up to the power house to have the steam turned off.

The Spongs were a canalling family on the C&O Canal in the early 20th century. Photo courtesy of the National Park Service.

The entire family was rushed to the hospital and their burns were treated. Sarah died four hours after the accident. John died at noon, and Willard passed away at 4:30 p.m. Nina's wounds weren't so bad, but she was in shock. Thomas and Samuel had minor wounds.

The police and public service commission opened investigations, and Coroner Nevitt visited the hospital to view the dead and toured the scene of the accident.

The coroner's inquest was held the following day. Virgil Walker, the night engineer, Rollins, and other company officials said that it was typical to blow off the steam from the boilers each morning.

"I knew of no danger in the world. I never saw the steam turned on there before in my life," Samuel testified.

In the end it was discovered that, although the company blew off steam from the boilers each morning, each boiler was done separately. That morning, Walker and Rollins had accidentally opened the valves on two different boilers at once. The added pressure in the pipe may have been enough to blow out the flange, which was found to have some corrosion that could have weakened it.

The company was found at fault for not providing a safe connection at the elbow of the pipe.

Samuel claimed the bodies of the dead children and rode with them on the Baltimore and Ohio Railroad to Keedysville, Md., on Sept. 13. They were buried in Mountain View Cemetery near Sharpsburg, Md., the following day.

"It was a most pathetic scene when the three little coffins were lowered into the graves. The funeral was exceptionally large. Hundreds of residents of the community witnessing the burial could not control their feeling and were forced to give vent to sorrow," the *Hagerstown Daily Mail* reported.

Samuel was able to attend the funeral, but Nina was still bed-bound in the hospital.

The following year Capital Traction paid the Spongs $5,000 (about $105,000 in today's dollars) in damages. The amount was for $1,500 for two of the children, $1,000 for the third child, and $1,000 for Nina's injuries.

Samuel Spong never boated on the C&O Canal again.

The grave marker for the Spong children in Mountain View Cemetery in Sharpsburg. Photo courtesy of Findagrave.com.

The Johnstown Flood's Cousin Nearly Killed the Canal

The C&O Canal was already struggling to stay afloat in the 1880s, but the Johnstown Flood put it under water.

On Memorial Day 1889, sixty-eight miles north of Cumberland, Md., the South Fork Dam on the Little Conemaugh River burst. Twenty million tons of water surged into the river to Johnstown, scraping much of the ground clean of trees, buildings, people and animals. More than 2,000 people were killed in the resulting flooding, one of the greatest disasters in American history. No one knew it at the time because the flooding knocked out telegraph lines at Johnstown.

The same weather system that set off the flooding in Johnstown also caused problems along the Potomac River.

"On Friday of last week the clouds began to come up from the Southeast, in thick, heavy masses, lowering until they seemed to roll over the mountains in dark, broad volumes. All day they continued to come, growing denser and swifter, and at three in the afternoon the showers came down, one after another with but slight intermission. Each succeeding downpour seemed heavier than the one before it. As night approached it could be seen that the Potomac river was rising rapidly; so, also, the Conococheague creek," according to the *Williamsport Transcript*.

Other reports said that a cyclone had entered the valley near Martinsburg, W. Va., moving north and crossing the Potomac River a few miles above Williamsport. It was followed by the heavy rains that caused the Potomac flooding.

The Johnstown Flood in 1889 left behind sunken canal boats. Photo courtesy of the National Park Service.

Men waited in the telephone office, evermore nervous as the river rose. They called to Cumberland, Md., asking about conditions there. The only report was that it was raining, but Cumberland was already experiencing its own problems.

"At five p.m. the entire city between Centre street and Will's creek on the one hand, between Bedford and Will's creek on another, and in South Cumberland as far down as the canal wharves, was under water to a depth varying from 6 inches to 8 feet," the *Cumberland Daily Times* reported.

The waters in both Wills Creek and the Potomac River rose steadily until 9 p.m. on Memorial Day.

Meanwhile, in Williamsport, "About ten at night, the torrents fell as though poured from a vast basin or reservoir in great dashes of water, and this continued - now pouring -

now letting up - shower upon shower - until long after midnight, when it finally ceased raining," according to the *Williamsport Transcript*.

Although the rain had stopped, the skies were still leaden and cloudy. When the residents awoke Saturday morning, they went outside to the knoll that overlooked the Potomac River. They saw that the river had crested its banks and flooded all of the low-lying land in town. It was now estimated that the Potomac River was a half a mile wide.

The flood of 1889 left behind damaged canal boats and a nearly destroyed C&O Canal. Photo courtesy of the National Park Service.

"The canal was no longer visible. The aqueduct at the mouth of the Conococheague could not be seen. Higher and higher rose the angry waters, sweeping onward with irresistible force, whirling and eddying, turbulent and restless, yet upon the surface seemingly smooth and calm," the *Williamsport Transcript* reported.

After the flood, the *Williamsport Transcript* reported that $30,000 worth of canal property had been "swept away."

As news of the flood spread, people came into Williamsport from other areas of the county to see the damage for themselves.

Williamsport, Md., after the flood of 1889. Photo courtesy of the National Park Service.

"The banks and hills were quickly lined with people, eagerly witnessing the scene before them. All sorts of articles float by; pulp from the pulp mill, seven miles above; barrels, tubs, casks, pieces of furniture, stacks of straw, logs of wood, green trees, torn up by the roots, cars, the debris of fallen buildings. Someone spies a huge, dark object, just coming 'round the bend, far up the river, and all eyes turn toward it. It proves to be a small house. Directly another appears, and another," according to the *Williamsport Transcript*.

Theodore Wolf and Charles Corby set out into the river to check the houses and thankfully, found them both vacant.

However, the sight testified to the power of the flood.

Then the Cumberland Valley Railroad Bridge crumbled and disappeared beneath the water.

This was the worst flood the area has seen to date, surpassing the highwater marks of the 1852 and 1877 floods.

The new Western Maryland Railroad Depot remained standing, but the water rose to the roof, making it an island in a widening river.

The *Williamsport Transcript* described another building being destroyed. "Crack! Crack! 'What is that?' The large paint house and store-house of the Chair Factory has moved off its foundations and turned toward the river. 'There it goes,' cry out a number of voices. Slowly it moves off with its cargo of newly-painted chairs - not to some port of trade, but to inevitable ruin. Now it strikes the aqueduct, and bursts asunder, part floating out into the main current, and part remaining against the bridge. Bundles of chairs float away."

The worst was yet to come as Wolf and Corby tried to salvage some of the furniture. On their way back to shore with their boats filled with chairs, Wolf fell out of the skiff and drowned. He was one of dozens of people killed during the flooding.

The water continued rising throughout the day, peaking around 4 p.m.

As the water receded over the next day, an even worse sight awaited the residents as the depth of the damage was revealed. Crop fields were covered in mud. Homes had been moved from their foundations or overturned.

"Joseph Shifflet and family, residing a short distance below this place, narrowly escaped drowning," according to the *Williamsport Transcript*. "The water was running rapidly around the house, and they just managed to escape in a boat before the house turned over and floated down the river."

Railroad cars at Williamsport nearly under water after the 1889 flood. Photo courtesy of the National Park Service.

As people assessed the damage to their homes and property, they felt that they could rebuild. The same could not be said for the canal. "Our present losses could be repaired in time, as they have been before, but it is doubtful if the canal, upon which our people are mainly dependent, will ever be repaired as a waterway," the *Williamsport Transcript* reported.

According to the *Historic Resource Study: Chesapeake and Ohio Canal,* the flood set new records all along the canal:

- Hancock, Md. – 3 feet above the previous record set in 1877.
- Williamsport – 7.5 feet above the 1877 record.
- Harpers Ferry, W.Va. – the water was 21 feet above the towpath and 2.8 above the rails on the B&O Railroad Bridge.
- Great Falls, Md. – the river rose 16 feet above the top surface of the coping on the dam and 4 feet higher than in the 1877 flood.

- Georgetown - 19.5 feet and 13.3 feet at the Potomac Aqueduct and Easby's Wharf in Georgetown respectively.

The *Baltimore Sun* published a report from F. H. Darby, stating, "From Cumberland to Georgetown, he said, there is not a point of settlement, where from thirty to forty families are in utter destination, and in need of immediate help. At Old Town, Hancock, Little Orleans, Four Locks, Williamsport, Sharpsburg, Mercerville, Harpers Ferry, Maryland side, Sandy Hook, Knoxville, Point of Rocks, Monocacy, Edward's Ferry, White's Ferry, Seneca and Great Falls, and all the country lying between these points, there is great suffering. Homes have been swept away, and the people have nothing left, not even clothing or furniture."

The final tallies from the flood damage along the Upper Potomac put it at 50 lives lost and more than $2 million in lost property.

"The loss by ruined bridges, washouts and land slides of the Western Division of the Baltimore & Ohio road reached more than half a million dollars.... The Western Maryland Railroad and its connecting lines, the Baltimore and Harrisburg and the Cumberland Valley roads were extensively damaged by washouts and destruction of bridges over a length of about sixty miles," according to *Appletons' Annual Cyclopedia and Register* (1889).

Reports from Superintendent Ed Mulvaney and J. P. Biser arrived at the canal company ten days after the flood. Needless to say, the damage was extensive from destroyed dams and breaks in the towpath to missing lockhouses and 1,200 cubic yards of mud at Georgetown. The damage to the canal was initially said to be between $500,000 and $1,000,000. That number was eventually lowered to $250,000 to $300,000.

The 1889 flood along the Potomac River caused $2 million in damage. Photo courtesy of the National Park Service.

The *Williamsport Transcript* reported, "Superintendent Mulvaney, of the Chesapeake and Ohio canal, arrived at Williamsport on Tuesday from Cumberland on an inspection tour. He reports the canal is in deplorable condition and the damages far in excess of those occasioned by the flood of 1877. There are numerous breaks and washouts between Williamsport and Cumberland, and the waterway lined and clogged up with all kinds of debris. He concedes the outlook to be gloomy for the maintenance of the canal, and in his opinion thinks it will be out of the question to restore it to use for navigation."

The *Hagerstown Mail* reported that Mulvaney told them, "A number of canal boats are washed out in the fields, and some of them badly damaged." He also estimated the flood damage to be twice that of the 1877 flood.

This was beyond the C&O Canal Company's ability to pay for. With that announcement, the canal as run by the canal company was dead. It would go into receivership with the B&O Railroad emerging as the receiver and essentially, the new owner of the canal.

The *Hagerstown Mail* compared the canal to a dead patient. "Upon its tombstone may be inscribed in a few words that, it died of politics and politicians … It was not the storm that killed the Canal—it could have recovered from the flood, had its recovery not been already rendered impossible by political blood poisoning."

The B&O and C&O: Rivals and Associates

The flood of 1889 put the Chesapeake and Ohio Canal out of business, at least the canal with which canallers were familiar. The flood not only damaged the canal, but it closed it so that there was no way for the company to even begin to generate income for the substantial repairs. Not that it would have helped, the company was deep in debt with no possibility of raising money to make repairs.

The C&O Canal Company directors wrote in a July 9, 1889, petition to the Maryland Board of Public Works that it was "impracticable to repair and operate the canal with any expectation that it can earn in the future revenue enough to keep itself a living and going concern."

On Dec., George S. Brown, James Sloan Jr., and Lloyd Lowndes, Jr., trustees for the 1844 bond holders filed a bill in the Circuit Court of Washington asking for the court to appoint receivers to take over the canal and operate it until the bondholders were paid.

Things then began to get confused because the 1844 bondholders weren't the only outstanding bonds on the canal. Bonds had been issued the year after the 1877 flood to pay for the canal's repairs from that flood. Those bondholders wanted their money, too, but they wanted to sell the canal.

On January 16, 1890, the bill for the 1844 bondholders was amended to include the 1878 bondholders.

"Possession of both the majority of the 1844 and 1878

bonds meant that the trustees held bonds that had mortgaged not just the future profits but also the real property and franchises of the company," according to canal historian Karen Gray in her article, "The C&O Canal Trusteeship 1890-1901." And the major bondholder in both instances was the canal's rival, the Baltimore and Ohio Railroad.

The Supreme Court of the District of Columbia appointed receivers for the canal on Jan. 29.

However, two days later, the Maryland courts became involved in the case and, along with the canal company, opposed the canal being placed in receivership. Their intention was that the property should be sold. They were joined in February with the minority share owners of the 1844 and 1878 bonds.

Washington County Judge A. H. Alvey appointed his own receivers to assess the condition of the canal, what it would cost to repair it, and what it would cost to operate following the repairs. The Washington-appointed receivers did the same thing.

"By Aug. 12, reports from all the receivers were filed, although the Maryland and the District Court receivers came to opposite decisions as to whether the canal could be operated in a manner that would produce adequate levels of revenue," Gray wrote.

At this point, some of the 1844 bondholders had second thoughts about selling the canal. They filed a petition saying that they were willing to pay to repair the canal and operate until not only the bonds were paid off but a profit was obtained for the bondholders, but they wanted to be able to select the receivers who would be in charge of this.

Alvey was ready to allow the sale of the canal when the 1844 bond trustees asked permission on Sept. 18 to redeem the 1878 bonds and they be allowed to restore and operate the canal. "The 1878 bondholders, chief among them the B&O Railroad, held a mortgage on the body of the canal; if the canal were sold, there would have been nothing for the 1844 bondholders," Elizabeth Kytle wrote in *Home on the Canal*.

Alvey issued an opinion on Oct. 2 that said he felt that it would be impractical to repair the canal and that it should be sold. He named trustees for the sale and how it would proceed. He then went on to suspend the sale to allow trustees of the 1848 bond, which were a small group of 1844 bondholders whose bonds hadn't sold by 1848, to repair and operate the canal until May 1, 1895. At that time, if the court wasn't satisfied with how much revenue it was producing, the sale would commence. "It is critical to recognize that this decree did not transfer ownership (i.e., title) of the C&O Canal Company and its property or earnings, but concerned control only," Gray wrote.

The bondholders who wanted the canal sold appealed the decision to the Maryland Court of Appeals, but the decision was upheld on February 20, 1891. Judge Robinson seemed to be willing to give the canal a chance to become profitable and if it didn't, the repairs made to it would make it a more attractive property on the auction block.

Robinson also wrote, "The suit was brought by the trustees at the request of a majority of the bondholders, and so long as they act in good faith, and for the purpose of carrying out the trust reposed in them under the mortgage, a minority bondholder has no right to interfere with them in the discharge of their duty."

The essence of all the legal entanglements was that the B&O Canal was in control of its rival. Kytle wrote that the financials arrangements "formed a labyrinth through which none but a dedicated financial historian would dare or care to grope." The problem was further complicated by the press reports that confused and misstated the legal status and responsibilities of the parties involves.

These actions were not taken directly by the B&O, which could not be done legally. It was done through trustees, which were appointed by the B&O as a bondholder.

The C&O Canal continued operating after the 1889 flood, but it did so in receivership and under the control of the B&O Railroad. Photo courtesy of the National Park Service.

The receivership era

The canal reopened for navigation near the beginning of September 1891.

However, it was still a struggle to make the canal a profitable venture. In December 1894, the B&O Railroad created the Chesapeake and Ohio Transportation Company of Washington County. According to the *Cumberland Evening Times*,

Construction of the Western Maryland Railroad as it was crossing the C&O Canal in 1907.

"The purposes of the corporation were to buy and lease lands, buy and transport timber, grain, fruits, seeds, &c., build boats and ships, mine coal, iron and other metals, open marble and slate quarries, operate canal boats by means of electricity, navigate the ocean by vessels, acquire bridges, wharves, &c., by lease or otherwise, and for other purposes." Its actual purpose appears to have been to create the illusion that the canal was operating at a profit so that it would remain open.

While the B&O Railroad had no great love for the canal, its existence was keeping the Western Maryland Railroad, which would have been a direct and strong competitor to the B&O, out of Western Maryland.

The canal trustees asked for extension of their ability to remain open based on being able to enter into a contract with the C&O Transportation Company with a guarantee of $100,000 in annual net revenues. Maryland and other bondholders argued against this, still preferring to sell the canal. However, the guarantee of revenue convinced the judge who allowed the canal to continue operating.

Because the plan was not based on a reality, the guarantee couldn't be met. "The financial picture for the C&O in the 1890s was mixed and the 'visionary' promises of the trustees and the C&OTC were unfulfilled. Although receipts exceeded expenditures from 1892 through 1896, the situation was reversed in the next three years," Gray wrote. Even the "profitable" years were only so on paper.

"In effect, the railroad lent the receivers money to repair the canal. It then formed a paper corporation through which the railroad furnished the canal company with funds to meet expenses and pay off loan from the railroad. Once having paid itself back, the railroad rewrote the contract, with court approval, to provide only that the canal be guaranteed its expenses," Kytle wrote.

As the finances turned south, so did the chances of selling the canal. The nationwide economic depression that had caused the deficit in the canal budget also hurt the B&O Railroad, which would have been the most likely buyer of the canal had it gone to auction.

The in 1902, the Consolidation Coal Company (which

was owned by the B&O Railroad) formed the Canal Towage Company. This is when canal life changed drastically for boatmen. The Canal Towage Company owned most of the boats operating on the canal and hired captains. They no longer worked independently.

In February 1904, the Western Maryland Railroad finally got its foot in the door when ten to fifteen miles of canal land that wasn't be used was condemned so that the railroad could build an extension. "The railroad also obtained permission to cross the canal at seven locations as well as to acquire canal land on the river side for the waste material from the rail line construction (on the berm)," Gray wrote.

Selling to the federal government

The floods of 1924 closed the C&O Canal for good. The B&O Railroad, which had lost the fight to keep the Western Maryland Railroad out of Western Maryland, had no desire to keep pouring money into the canal. It was having its own financial troubles. It had even used the canal as collateral to secure a loan from the federal government's Reconstruction Finance Corporation.

The receivers kept the canal technically operating since it was still supplying water to Georgetown businesses along the canal. Their position was that the canal had not been abandoned, only closed because there was not enough business.

When the railroad couldn't pay a $2 million note to the federal government in 1938, the railroad foreclosed on the canal even though it did not own the canal. It only had a financial interest in a portion of it. However, the railroad was able to take possession of the canal, thus cutting out all of the other bondholders and leaving them with nothing.

The B&O sold the canal to the government for $2 million. "It was all a paper transfer, no money changed hands, and it took place almost in the blink of an eye," Kytle wrote.

The railroad then used its reduced liabilities to leverage even another loan from the federal government in the amount of $8.2 million.

Questions still exist today as to financial entanglements between the canal and railroad and whether the actions taken were actually legal.

Although the federal government bought the C&O Canal in 1938, it didn't become a national park until 1971. Photo courtesy of the National Park Service.

When the C&O Canal Closed

When Pat Boyer docked his Canal Towage Company boat No. 5 in the Cumberland basin of the Chesapeake and Ohio Canal near the end of November 1923, he didn't know he was marking the end of an era. He had dropped off a load of coal in Georgetown and made it back to Cumberland before the canal was drained for the winter. With No. 5 already in the basin, Boyer would be one of the first boats loaded when once next spring came and the boating season started.

Next spring came, but the boating season didn't.

What did come was rain. On March 28 and 29, 1924, heavy rains pelted the area helping to melt the snow on the mountains. All that melted snow and rain ran into the creeks and Potomac River.

"By 8:30 a.m. on the 29th, Wills Creek overflowed its banks resulting in tremendous havoc and property loss in the Cumberland vicinity. Telephone, telegraph and electric wires were swept away and the city left in darkness. Cumberland's central business district was flooded to a height of four feet. Most of the paving washed away with a torrent of water rushing down Mechanic Street at a great velocity," wrote local historian Al Feldstein in the historical commentary of the novel *The Rain Man*.

Contemporary newspaper reports said the waters were rising as fast as thirty inches an hour and approaching the then-record crest of the 1889 flood that had helped put the canal's rival, the Baltimore and Ohio Railroad, in control of it when the canal went into receivership.

When the 1924 floodwaters receded, the damage was assessed. "There was really little destruction outside of the canal, which had been badly mauled at Cumberland where the torrent in the river had leveled some of the banks. The dams survived the onslaught of the river fairly well, and the lower valley escaped serious damage altogether," wrote Walter Sanderlin in *The Great National Project*.

When the C&O Canal closed in 1924, a way of life disappeared. Photo courtesy of the National Park Service.

While the canal could have been repaired as it had been after previous floods, the B&O Railroad Company chose not to do so. The canal was a burden to railroad company. The B&O Railroad had needed control of the canal rights of way to hinder the westward expansion of the Western Maryland Railroad. The courts had that had given the railroad control of the canal had also ordered that the canal needed to operate the canal profitably or lose its charter. With only about $50,000 a year being collected in tolls, Mike High wrote in *The C&O Canal Companion* that the B&O Railroad was "most assuredly not fulfilling the court's stipulation that it continue to show a profit to hold its charter."

Canaller George Hooper Wolfe, wrote in *I Drove Mules on the C&O Canal*, "The railroad saw in this an opportunity to relieve itself of the expense of further operation. Enough repairs were made to assert that the Canal was a going concern, with enough revenues from the Georgetown factories and dams along the river to pay the expenses of a minimum operating staff; and it was also maintained that the Canal could be placed in operation quickly if business warranted. The court went along with this fiction, and the B&O retained the property, but without having any further expenses for its maintenance."

The canal had been dying for years. The B&O Railroad had kept it going for other reasons.

In a 1979 interview featured in *Home on the Canal*, Lester Mose, Sr. who had worked on the canal during its last years, said, "It could be that something else interfered with them; but in '22 the canal didn't do much, and in '23 they done very little. I worked at Pinesburg and I was out there right along the canal and I could walk out there and look at it. Once in a while you'd see a boat go by, but not too many."

Some boats hauled sand from Georgetown to the power plant that was being constructed in Williamsport for a few months in 1924, but the damage at the Cumberland end kept boats away. Boyer's No. 5 had been the last boat to haul freight on the canal.

Mose said, "The '24 flood took all the boats away. What wasn't taken away in '24 [the] '36 [flood] cleaned them up. There wasn't nothing there. It was dead. Closed up and growed up with trees."

The canal had originally reached Cumberland in 1850 and it ended there unintentionally because of competition from the B&O Railroad and an intentional decision by the railroad.

The B&O Railroad sold its rights to the canal to the federal government in August 1938 for $2 million. It was a paper transaction that allowed the railroad to pay off some of its $80 million loan from the federal government's Reconstruction Finance Corp and to borrow another $8.2 million more.

Otho Swain was born on the canal in 1901 and worked on it during its final years. He said in a 1976 interview, "The canal finally closed down in 1924. There was flood damage then, but the railroad—it was the railroad that really killed the canal."

A canal boat left abandoned after the C&O Canal closed in 1924. Photo courtesy of the National Park Service.

Once the Canal Closed

The Murders That Didn't Happen on the Canal

Canallers were surprised one morning in the late 1890's as they exited the somewhat frightening Paw Paw Tunnel only to meet a sight of true horror.

The lockhouse at lock 64 2/3 just below the east end of the tunnel was a charred mess. It had burned to the ground during the night and it was probably just by luck that it hadn't started a forest fire.

The first canallers on the scene went ashore to search for the lock keeper. He was a friendly man who lived alone in the house and tended the five locks—61, 62, 63 1/3, 64 2/3 and 66—at the east end of the tunnel.

Another lock had originally been planned in that group of locks, but financial difficulties forced the C&O Canal Company to drop the plan for lock 65 and renumber the locks around it, which is why two of the locks had fractions in their number.

According to George Hooper Wolfe in his book, *I Drove Mules on the C&O Canal*, the lockkeeper "was found in the ruins, dead of burns and crushed skull, evidently murdered."

Because of the isolation of the area, word of the crime had to be sent back to Paw Paw, W.Va., which was the nearest town more than a mile away. From Paw Paw, a telegram could be sent to Cumberland to get the Allegany County sheriff down to the scene. It all took the better part of a day.

Because of the difficulty required in reaching the lock

house, the murderer had to know that something was there that he wanted.

Wolfe wrote that the lock keeper "was a collector of rare and unusual coins and delighted in showing them to Canal boatmen and anyone else interested. Many of the Canal boatmen would pick up coins for him as he was well liked by those who knew him."

The eastern end of the Paw Paw Tunnel. It was near here that a brutal murder was supposed to have occurred. Photo courtesy of the Library of Congress.

As search of the house's ruins showed that the coins were missing, but the sheriff was unable to find a clue as to who had committed the murder.

"The incident was just about forgotten and people heard rumors that the affair was probably a local, well-planned inside job," Wolfe wrote.

However, the canallers were reminded each time they

passed through the tunnel locks of the friend whom they had lost. They also remembered some of the coins in the lock-keeper's collection. Some they had found for their friend and others were unusual enough to stick in their memories.

Months after the murder, some canallers were in one of Shantytown's many saloons closing the place down. A stranger walked in and offered to buy the canallers a drink, which they readily accepted. When the stranger paid for the drinks, he used a coin that the canallers recognized as one of the missing coins from the lockkeeper's collection.

"The boatmen took the stranger in hand, searched him, and found other coins that had been shown to them by the locktender many times before. The boatmen handled him roughly and would have killed him on the spot had not the barkeeper interfered," Wolfe wrote.

Police were called to arrest the stranger. At his trial, canallers testified to which coins had come from the dead lock keeper's collection and businessmen testified that the stranger had tried to pass other rare coins at their shops.

"On this evidence he was found guilty and hanged, maintaining his innocence, but finally admitting his guilt in the end," Wolfe wrote.

That's how the story goes of the murder on the C&O Canal, and thanks to the popularity of Wolfe's book, most people accept it as the truth. However, Wolfe wrote his book recalling his days on the canal in 1969 at age 75, and the real story didn't unfold quite the way he remembered it.

Trying to verify Wolfe's story is hard because it was vague. No names are given and only a decade is mentioned as a time frame for the murders. The C&O Canal park rangers don't believe the story, but they do tell a story of another murder on the canal that is better sourced.

"Lock tender Joe Davis and his wife were murdered here

by shooting in 1934," Thomas Hahn wrote in his *Towpath Guide.* He expanded on the story in *The Chesapeake & Ohio Canal Lock-Houses & Lock-Keepers*, writing that Davis took care of Lock 61 in the last decades of the canal's operation. Hahn wrote that the bodies of Davis and his wife were burned after the murder to try and cover up the crime.

The first thing that caught my attention was the location of both murders. The two lockhouses were only 1.5 miles apart along an isolated section of the canal. What was the likelihood that three people were murdered and burned there?

Or was it five?

A canal boat passing through a lock. Photo courtesy of the National Park Service.

Searching the newspapers brings up a headline in the August 5, 1830, *Hagerstown Morning Herald.* It announced, "Two Believed Burned in Allegany Co. Home - FOUL PLAY IS HINTED AFTER SKULLS FOUND - Mystery Marks Home Burning And Disappearance At Kifer". This headline set the narrative that became the urban legend. However, the facts told a different story.

This turns out to be the Joseph Davis story, so Hahn has the year wrong in his account (which he admits is second-hand information).

Joseph Davis and his wife were killed in a fire on Aug. 4. "They were found on the springs of a bed in the ruins of the house. Two skulls crumbled when touched," the *Morning Herald* reported. The fire was so hot that the newspaper reported that not only had the wood burned in the house but so had the locks and hardware.

Newspaper reports said that Mrs. Davis' name was Allie, but the 1930 census reported it as Ella. The newspaper accounts also vary on both of the Davis's ages. According to the 1930 census, Joseph was 59 and Ella was 53.

The Davis's bones were found in the basement of the house where they had fallen once the floor had collapsed. Ella Davis was identified by her wedding ring.

A neighbor, drawn by the smoke, found the ruins of the house the day after the fire and reported it to the authorities. The bones that were found were initially taken to Paw Paw, W.Va., which was the nearest town of any size. State's Attorney William Huster, Allegany County Sheriff W. H. Harvey and Coroner Joseph Finan came from Cumberland to investigate the case and determine what happened.

The newspaper also reported that casings from a small-caliber gun were also found near the body.

Davis had been a lockkeeper at Lock 61 on the canal, but since the canal had shut down six years previously, he reported to the census that he was a farmer. It is not mentioned in the article whether he and Ella were still living in the lock-house, but it is possible.

Though the murder story spread quickly through the community, the authorities quickly abandoned the idea.

"It had been rumored that the couple had met with foul

play and their bodies burned in their home to conceal the crime. This was based on a report that old coins which Davis collected and had under glass in a frame was missing. The officers, however, found a five-dollar gold piece and the metal of twelve silver coins, which had melted," the *Hagerstown Daily Mail* reported on the afternoon of Aug. 5.

The story of the missing coins is similar to Wolfe's story.

Finan announced on Aug. 6 that Joseph Davis had been smoking, probably a pipe, and may have fallen asleep. A spark from the house caught the house on fire. No foul play was suspected.

Even this story has evolved. When I originally published the story in 2013, it was a recounting of the Wolfe story. Then at the urging of Karen Gray, a C&O Canal historian, I looked into the Davis murder and was able to reconcile the two stories.

In 2015, Gray wrote me that she had found another murder that seemed to tie into the canal legends.

In 1900, William McCully lived along the canal near the eastern end of the Paw Paw Tunnel. Although this is where the Lockhouses 61-64 were located, McCully was not a lockkeeper. He ran a mercantile business near the tunnel that catered canallers.

When McCully died in 1903, the *Cumberland Evening Times* reported, "About three years ago the deceased and his aged wife were the victims of horrible treatment by a gang of robber, who, after tying them both with rope, applied torches to their feet until they revealed where a considerable sum of money was hidden."

When the couple was discovered the next morning, it was thought that they would die. Mrs. McCully never did recover fully from the robbery and died three months later.

Sound familiar? Robbers stealing money and the use of

fire. Wolfe's story now seems a poor recollection that combines the McCully and Davis stories although there are significant differences between this story and the others. There was no murder and no arson, the location and date would suggest that it influenced the legend of the canal murder.

"This has got to be one of the best examples of how legends reflect and rework true or likely true information from diverse sources," Gray wrote to me.

Forging Through the Mountains

When the Chesapeake and Ohio Canal finally opened to Cumberland, Md., in 1850, the canal directors still talked of continuing on to the Ohio River so that boats could travel from Washington, D.C., to Pittsburgh, Pa. This was the ultimate goal of the canal, which is why it was named what it was.

However, nothing ever came of finishing the canal, and it closed in 1924. A few years later, the U.S. Army Corps of Engineers took another look at the canal and the Potomac River.

At the beginning of 1938, it was announced that the Army Corps of Engineers had completed its survey of the river and its tributaries "for a proposed canalized waterway from Washington to Cumberland and connecting with the Ohio River at Pittsburgh with tidewater," according to the *Oakland Republican*.

The C&O Canal had been closed for 14 years at this point and had fallen into disrepair, with lock doors missing, the berm damaged, and trees growing in the canal. In addition, in its final years, the canal had been too narrow and shallow for the increasing size of cargo ships.

The Army Corps of Engineers survey decided not to use the existing canal but to turn the Potomac River into a navigable waterway. It was revealed that to canalize the Potomac River to Cumberland would require 27 dams, "four of them to be power-navigation dams capable of supplying

1,000,000,000 kilowatt hours of prime power annually," according to the newspaper.

The C&O Canal in Georgetown after it had closed. Photo courtesy of the Library of Congress.

The construction cost was estimated at $60 million ($1.01 billion in 2017 dollars). This would also pay for creating a twelve-foot-channel in the Potomac River from Washington,

D.C. to Cumberland. "A nine-foot water-way tunnel is proposed under the mountains to the Youghiogheny river, then through three locks and dams to the mouth of that stream at McKeesport with the Monongahela River," according to the newspaper.

The tunnel, which would have started near West Newton, Pa., was declared feasible and a better alternative than building a series of locks and dams to take canal boats up and over the mountains.

Engineers worked out of Cumberland and Eastern Garrett County in Maryland for a number of years looking at factors such as navigation, water power, flood control, and irrigation.

Four routes leaving Cumberland on existing waterways were considered. These were Will's Creek and the Casselman River; Savage River via Piney Creek or the Casselman River; Deep Creek and the Youghiogheny River; or the North Branch Potomac River and Youghiogheny River.

Once the engineers' report was released, businesspeople to the west of the mountains began considering its possibilities as well as the politicians in these areas. In particular, coal and iron producers in the Pittsburgh area studied the proposed plan. It would offer them a new way to get their products to Washington, D. C.

Politicians to the west of the mountains supported the idea and a hearing was scheduled. The Western Pennsylvania politicians urged businessmen and citizens to attend and voice their opinions. They released a statement that read, in part: "The present fate of this much needed improvement rests with those in Western Pennsylvania, who are vitally interested."

Despite the initial interest, the plan eventually stalled before any further money was allocated.

In part, this was due to the fact that by June of 1938, an

agreement was reached whereby the Baltimore and Ohio Railroad sold its holdings in the canal to the Public Works Administration, which in turn, would give the property to the National Park Service.

"It is understood that the national park services plan to use the right of way for scenic highway, as far west as Great Falls, and eventually all the way to this city," *The Cumberland Evening Times* reported.

This was the plan until U.S. Supreme Court Justice William O. Douglas hiked the towpath with a group of citizens and reporters in 1954 in an effort to save the C&O Canal. The hike changed the opinion of some of the newspaper editors who had been supporting the parkway.

In 1971, the C&O Canal finally became a National Historic Park.

The Connection Between the JFK Assassination and the C&O Canal

On October 12, 1964, artist Mary Pinchot Meyer, 43, finished her latest painting. While it was drying, she dressed in warm clothes and went out for an afternoon walk along the Chesapeake and Ohio Canal towpath. Living in Georgetown, afternoon walks on the canal were part of her daily routine.

According to Ben Hayes in his article, "The Death of Mary Pinchot Meyer," Air Force Lieutenant William Mitchell was running along the towpath that day. He told police that he had passed two people during his run. One was a woman whose description matched Meyer's. The other person was a man walking about 200 yards behind the woman. "Mitchell described the man as being about the same height as him, and 'wearing a light colored wind breaker, dark slacks, and a peaked golf hat,'" Hayes wrote.

Henry Wiggins was an Esso station employee on a service call to jump start a car with a dead battery. He heard a person from the direction of the towpath yell, "Someone help me! Someone help me!"

Then he heard two shots. He ran to a wall that overlooked the towpath. He saw "a black man in a light jacket, dark slacks, and a dark cap standing over the body of a white woman…" Phillip Nobilem and Ron Rosenbaum wrote in their article, "The Circus Aftermath of JFK's Best and Brightest Affair." The man put a dark object in his pocket and hurried into the woods between the towpath and the Potomac River. Wiggins hurried back to the Esso station and called the police.

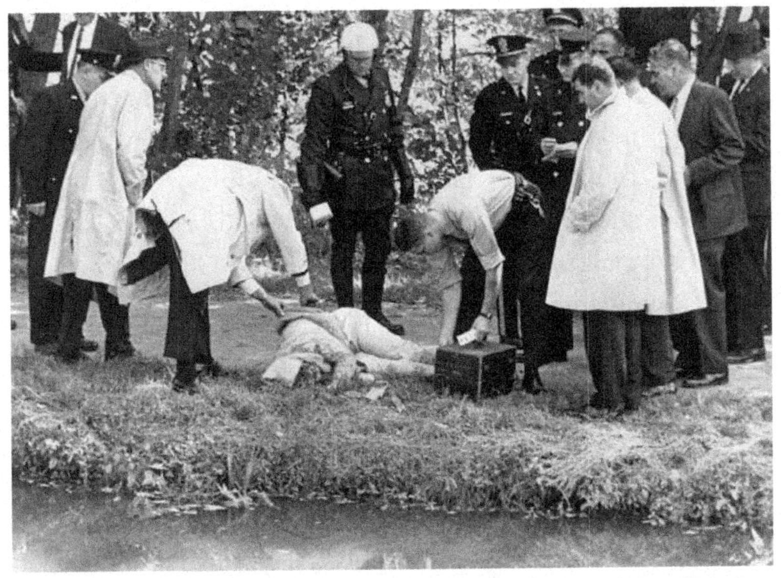

Police surround Mary Pinchot Meyer's body on the C&O Canal towpath.

As a cub reporter for the *Washington Star*, Lance Morrow spent a lot time in the pressroom at the police headquarters. He heard the call dispatching patrol cars to a murder scene and rushed to the scene. He had played on the canal as a boy and knew his way around it. He was able to reach the body before even the police arrived.

He wrote, "She lay on her side, as if sleeping. She was dressed in a light blue fluffy angora sweater, pedal pushers and sneakers. ... I saw a neat and almost bloodless bullet hole in her head. She looked entirely peaceful, vaguely patrician. She had an air of Georgetown."

The police sealed off all of the nearby exits from the towpath and began a manhunt of the area. The only person they found was an African American man named Ray Crump, Jr. When the police found him, he was dripping wet and wearing dark slacks and a peaked golf cap. He had no jacket and his zipper was open. "Crump said he had gotten wet when he lost his fishing pole and went into the river to try and retrieve it," Hayes wrote. "Moments later, when Crump was showing Officer Warner where he claimed to be fishing, Henry Wiggins saw the two of them down by the river and started yelling to police that that was the man he saw kill Mary Meyer."

Mary Pinchot Meyer

Crump was arrested.

As the investigation continued, the area was searched for evidence. No murder weapon was ever found, but a white windbreaker was found near the murder site. Not only did it fit Crump well, but his wife identified it as being her husband's. While questioning Crump's wife, Police saw Crump's fishing tackle in his hall closet. When neighbors were questions, they told the police that they had seen Crump leaving that morning wearing a white windbreaker and carrying no fishing tackle.

While the circumstantial case against Crump seemed strong, his defense attorney was able to create plenty of reasonable doubt for the jury. It deliberated for eleven hours and remained deadlocked. Crump was acquitted.

Meyer's case was officially closed, but it remains unsolved.

For most people, Meyer's murder was just another one of the many unsolved homicides in Washington, D.C. It wasn't until years later that it was discovered who Meyer was and what happened right after she was murdered.

The truth started to come out in a 1976 article in the *National Enquirer*. "Enquirer articles rarely carry much weight, but the basic content of that article has since been confirmed by those involved," Hayes wrote.

Meyer's ex-husband was Cord Meyer, a WWII vet who also happened to be in charge of the CIA's clandestine services. Her brother-in-law was Ben Bradlee who wrote for *Newsweek* at the time. The most-shocking revelation about Meyer, though, was that she had had a two-year affair with President John F. Kennedy.

Peter Janney is the author of *Mary's Mosaic: The CIA Conspiracy to Murder John F. Kennedy, Mary Pinchot Meyer, and Their Vision of World Peace*. Besides speculating that Meyer may have been killed because she discovered something about Kennedy's assassination, Janney wrote that Kennedy and Meyer shared marijuana and LSD during their meetings. He also said that she encouraged Kennedy to seek peaceful solutions to world crises.

Bradlee wrote in his book, *A Good Life*, that Meyer's best friend Ann Truitt called from Tokyo upon learning of her friend's death. She expressed her condolences, and then told the Bradlees that Meyer had kept a personal journal and had asked Truitt to retrieve it "if anything ever happened to me."

Truitt asked if the Bradlees had found it, but they hadn't even started going through Meyer's belongings. Her house was only a few blocks away so Bradlee and his wife walked over the next morning.

President John F. Kennedy and Mary Pinchot Meyer.

"It was locked, as we had expected, but when we got inside, we found Jim Angleton, and to our complete surprise he told us he, too, was looking for Mary's diary," Bradlee wrote.

Angleton explained his wife, Cicely, had also been asked by Meyer to retrieve the diary if something happened to her. Hayes wrote that some accounts also say that Cord Meyer was involved. Whether it was Cord Meyer or Angleton, it appears as if the CIA may have taken an interest in Meyer's journal.

Meyer's sister, Tony Bradlee, found the journal that afternoon. "Upon reading through it, they found a short section that discussed an affair between Mary and an unnamed person," Hayes wrote. "Despite the anonymity, it was obviously the President of the United States."

The Bradlees gave the diary to Angleton to destroy, but he didn't. When the Bradlees discovered this, they retrieved the journal and destroyed it themselves.

So did Morrow meet her end on the C&O Canal towpath because she knew too much about Kennedy's assassination? Most people would say, "no," but there are still unanswered questions about her death and some questionable connections.

Rethinking the C&O Canal

The old saying goes, "You can't fit a square peg in a round hole." Yet for more than ninety years, historians have said that somehow ninety-two-foot-long canal boats on the Chesapeake and Ohio Canal fit into locks that could hold boats no larger than ninety feet and probably less.

It's just one of the many questions that modern researchers are finding need to be answered about the C&O Canal. Some have easy answers that go against the accepted history of the canal. Others, like the question of canal-boat length, are still being researched.

Both have historians and National Park Service staff rethinking how the C&O Canal operated.

The C&O Canal ended business operations in 1924. Since then, books have been written about the canal, historians have researched the lives of canallers and lock tenders, and the National Park Service has documented the life of the canal. You would think that in that time, all that could be known about the canal had been discovered. It turns out that that's not the case.

"New information available and things are happening remarkably quickly," said Karen Gray, a C&O Canal National Historical Park historian.

The work being done is the transcription of canal records, historic newspaper articles, and other canal documents, primarily by William Bauman, a member of the C&O Canal Association. Gray vets a lot of the information. Some pieces are posted on the C&O Canal NPS site, but she puts most of the information on the C&O Canal Association web site in the "Canal History" section. The section includes oral histories, newspaper reports from long-forgotten newspapers along the canal, books, reports, payroll records, canal boat registration documents, and family histories.

"William Bauman has done a lot of terrific work collecting and transcribing records and articles to give everyone a flavor of how the canal operated," said Bill Holdsworth, who is both the president and webmaster for the C&O Canal Association.

The C&O Canal Association is a volunteer organization that promotes and advocates for the canal.

"There's so much available, but it needs to data mined," Gray said.

A careful reading of this new information has turned some long-held beliefs about the canal on their heads.

For instance, it has been written that canal boats in the 1800s were privately owned and often operated by a family. While they often were privately owned, "It was written into the boat mortgages that the boat needed to operate 24 hours a day," Gray said. "A family is not going to be able to do that."

Holdsworth said this is the most-surprising thing that he has learned from the new information. "Canal work was not this leisurely, bucolic life of strolling along the towpath," he said. "Those people were working hard and moving fast along the towpath."

Records show canallers were making the trip along the canal in roughly four days.

Gray explained that the idea of family run boats comes primarily from a 1923 U.S. Department of Labor study that was conducted at a time when 60 percent of the canal boats were run by a family.

In addition to boats not being family run, evidence suggests that a single captain might have been in charge of up to four boats. What is not certain at this time is whether those boats moved together or one towed another boat or some other variation, but the records don't support the one boat – one captain idea.

The lock at the Great Falls Tavern Visitor Center on the C&O Canal.

"It's really clear that we need to rethink our original beliefs of how the canal operated," Gray said.

In her own study, she divides the canal into the three periods. The first period is the time up until the canal opened to Cumberland. During this point, the canal was being built, but it had partial operation to different types of boats. From 1850 to the turn of the century, the canal operated independently for the most part and also had its golden age. From the turn of the century until the canal closed, it operated primarily under the Canal Towage Company at a reduced capacity.

The research has even turned up a couple mysteries that have yet to be solved.

Before the canal was fully completed to Cumberland in 1850, flatbed riverboats used to travel the Potomac River and enter the partially open canal at the dam near Williamsport. From there, they could continue their journey to Georgetown.

The question is how did they continue their journey? Riverboats were carried by the current with the crew using poles to guide the boat. Poles could not be used on the canal, though, or the clay berm would have been damaged. So how were the boats moved through the canal?

"Most likely, someone rented mules at Williamsport, but we don't know for sure," Gray said.

Perhaps the biggest mystery is how canal boats that were supposed to be ninety-two-feet long fit into some locks that could hold boats no longer eighty-five to ninety feet. The ninety-two-foot boat length comes from a single boat that was used to make drawings from. At the time the drawings were made, the boat had been out of the water for years so it is probable that frame may have loosened somewhat, adding length and width to the dimensions. This is only a guess at this time, though.

A National Park Service employee acts as a mule walker along the C&O Canal at the Great Falls Tavern Visitors Center.

"All of this information is a great resource that we've been able to make available to the world so that future researchers and future students can did down an do deep analysis," Holdsworth said.

He said that since much of the current beliefs about the canal come from oral histories of canallers and information from the canal's last days, this new information is changing people's impressions of the canal.

Catherine Bragaw, chief of interpretation for the C&O Canal, said that rangers are always looking for stories that people can relate to and that as more research becomes available, it may change the stories.

"It's not unusual for history to change," Bragaw said. "Some history stays consistent. Some is dynamic as more is uncovered."

She said that interpretation is an art because different people can focus on different aspects of the subject. That, in turn, affects, the stories and information they incorporate into their presentations.

"It's fascinating to unlock the mysteries," Bragaw said.

That's just what this new research continues to do. It is unlocking the mysteries of the early days of the canal and discovering new ones that need to be solved.

Acknowledgements

I wanted to thank all of those people who helped me put the *Secrets of the C&O Canal: Little-Known Stories & Hidden History Along the Potomac River* together. I've been enjoying writing the Secrets series, but more goes into this series than simply writing.

Throughout history the metaphor of being able to see further if you stand on the shoulders of giants has been used time and again. It's applicable here as well.

The reason that I'm able to write these books, in part, is because others who share my interest in the canal have researched just about every aspect of it. They have shared their findings in articles and on the Internet. It's using this basis of research that I've been able to find stories that I feel will appeal to you as the reader. They have certainly caught my attention.

Also, I'm not done using the Chesapeake and Ohio Canal as a setting in both my fiction and nonfiction writing. I'm not sure when I'll come back to it, but I know I will. I love the canal.

Two of the biggest giants that have helped me over the years have been Karen Gray with the C&O Canal National Park and the multitude of volunteer researchers with the C&O Canal Association. The former group transcribes many of the historical documents and newspaper articles about the canal and posts them on the association's web site where people like me can read them.

Also, I'd like to thank Grace Eyler for another great-looking cover. She is a talented designer who helps make my books eye catching.

I have probably missed someone who I'll remember after this book goes to print. If so, it's not because I didn't appreciate your input, it's because, as my sons would tell me, that I'm forgetting things in my old age.

James Rada, Jr.
January 30, 2018

About the Author

James Rada, Jr. has written many works of historical fiction and non-fiction history. They include the popular books *Saving Shallmar: Christmas Spirit in a Coal Town*, *Canawlers*, and *Battlefield Angels: The Daughters of Charity Work as Civil War Nurses*.

He lives in Gettysburg, Pa., where he works as a freelance writer. James has received numerous awards from the Maryland-Delaware-DC Press Association, Associated Press, Maryland State Teachers Association, Society of Professional Journalists, and Community Newspapers Holdings, Inc. for his newspaper writing.

If you would like to be kept up to date on new books being published by James or ask him questions, he can be reached by e-mail at *jimrada@yahoo.com.*

To see James' other books or to order copies on-line, go to *www.jamesrada.com.*

PLEASE LEAVE A REVIEW

If you enjoyed this book, please help other readers find it. Reviews help the author get more exposure for his books. Please take a few minutes to review this book at *Amazon.com* or *Goodreads.com.* Thank you, and if you sign up for my mailing list at *jamesrada.com*, you can get FREE ebooks.

How Many Secrets Do You Know?

Secrets of Garrett County: Little-Known Stories & Hidden History from Maryland's Westernmost County

Known for its natural beauty, Garrett County is made up of interesting people, places, and events that make it unique. From the time the CIA poisoned people with LSD at Deep Creek Lake to the story of the Black Widow Murderess of Grantsville, these stories will intrigue you. *Secrets of Garrett County* includes 44 fascinating stories and 58 pictures.

Secrets of Catoctin Mountain County: Little-Known Stories & Hidden History from Frederick & Loudoun Counties

Catoctin Mountain runs from Maryland to Virginia, crossing the Potomac River as it does. Its history dates back to prehistoric times and is filled with story of crimes, secrets, monsters and drama. From the legendary snallygaster monster to the WWII spy training camp, these stories will intrigue you. *Secrets of Catoctin Mountain* includes 29 fascinating stories and 64 pictures.

Visit *www.jamesrada.com* for updates on author signings, presentations, & classes. You can also find out how to download three historical novels for FREE.

Available wherever books are sold.

Made in the USA
Middletown, DE
13 September 2019